elena's fiesta recipes

elena's
fiesta recipes

BY ELENA ZELAYETA

FOREWORD BY HELEN EVANS BROWN

COMMENTARIES BY MARKA RITCHIE

WARD RITCHIE PRESS · PASADENA

Lithographed in the United States

Design by Ward Ritchie

With love and gratitude to Lou Richardson and Genevieve Callahan, whose friendship has been so inspiring.

contents

&❧ *Elena wishes to thank General Mills Incorporated and International Mineral and Chemical Corporation (Ac'cent) for permission to use recipes included in this book.*

vii

FOREWORD

To know Elena Zelayeta is to have a favorite friend,
to know a very special person. Elena of the gay laugh,
the nimble fingers, the quick wit . . . Elena who has
thousands of friends and sees none of them.

This book is not a Mexican cook book. It is *Elena's*
book—her second cook book, third book. The recipes are
all hers; the credit for setting them on paper goes to
Marka Ritchie, whose knowledge of Spanish, ability as a
cook, and sense of humor have added much charm
to this book. Jessica McLachlin, of The Wine Institute,
has also worked hard on the project. A friend of
everyone, but particularly of Elena, she spent many
hours checking the finished manuscript. My part
has been to kibitz in Elena's kitchen, to taste of her
wonderful food, to introduce her to you who may not
know her. Fun, all of it, but anything to do
with Elena is fun.

Her first cook book, *Elena's Famous Mexican and
Spanish Recipes*, is just that. The fact that Elena herself
has sold over 90,000 copies of the book is proof of
its worth, of the fact that no one interested in fine
Mexican food should be without it. *This* book is also aptly

named *Elena's Fiesta Recipes*—gay festive recipes for
the meals that Elena serves her friends and family.
They are party recipes—for any meal at Elena's is a
party—but seldom expensive, never fussy ones. Many of
the dishes are American, some with just a hint of
Spanish accent. Others are frankly Mexican, straight
from the land of Elena's birth. Some are inspired by
Spain, whence her parents came, and a few are from
Elena's other book—recipes so in demand that we dared
not omit them here. But all of them are *Elena's* recipes
and all have that inimitable touch that is Elena.

It is natural that many of Elena's recipes have a
Mexican flavor, many more a taste of Spain. She herself
wants you to know that the two are *very*, *very* different.
Masa, the corn paste that is the backbone of Mexican
food—of the tortilla, the tamale, the enchilada—is
not used in Spain. Rice is apt to supplant it. In Spain
saffron and olive oil, tomato and onions are omnipresent,
while in Mexico it is the chile pepper, the bean,
oregano, coriander, and cuminos that perfume the
cocina. Elena says that Mexican recipes need not be
blazing with hot peppers. Certainly hers, concocted for
her American sons and her American friends, are not.
(Just as some of us have an occasional childhood longing
for a jelly bean or licorice whip, so Elena sometimes
craves something fiercely hot. She cures this nostalgia
with an ardent snack—a taste of salsa Jalapeña or
perhaps chiles curtidos.)

Elena's friends remember that she is blind only when
she asks to have a letter read, an elusive jar of spice
located. For the most part she bounces around the
kitchen with an energy and an assurance that puts the
rest of us to shame. Marka and I, though both reasonably
adept in the kitchen, felt like a couple of fearful
and clumsy rookies when we tried to heat tortillas under

Elena's tutelage. "Just put the tortilla on the lighted burner," said Elena, "and keep turning it so that it won't burn." She herself did just that, and with her bare hands; she chatted merrily as she unconcernedly kept the tortillas moving. Marka, braver than I, tried first, and Elena burst into howls of glee at her attempt. "Mariquita, what are you afraid of? You are doing it too slowly." Elena not only cooks by ear, she *listens* to other people's cooking—she could hear Marka's cautious snatches at the hot tortilla. When my turn came, I used the tongs. Elena was enough of a lady to pretend that she didn't know that I cheated.

Not only is Elena a superlative cook, she is the best kitchen manager I know. This is due partly to her past experience in the restaurant business, but mostly to the fact that she has compensated for her lack of vision by a foresight that might well be emulated by the rest of us. Her simplification of cooking and her ability to organize a meal are remarkable. Everything that can be done ahead of time is done, everything that requires last-minute attention is so planned that that attention is of the briefest. Elena can greet her guests and relax with them before dinner as if she had a kitchen full of help. And then, miraculously, she will announce that dinner is served. And it is—beautifully, deliciously served.

I cannot play favorites with Elena's recipes. Always, the last one I have tasted is the best. Better that you try them. There are Chuletas—thin tender little patties of meat, served hot with an exquisite cold sauce. There are Carnitas—hot succulent cubes of crisp pork that, as an appetizer, will have both trenchermen and gastronomes in a happy dither. There are Elena's Chiles Rellenos, Elena's North-of-the-Border version created to pamper American palates, and Minguiches—

a glorious concoction of French pancakes, spinach, sour cream and tangy Jack cheese—a recipe that any Continental chef would gladly claim. There are soups and salads, entrées and desserts, every one of them a joy to cook and a delight to serve. And serve them generously. "Remember," Elena says, "a full belly makes a happy heart."

HELEN EVANS BROWN

fOREWORD

TO THE REVISED EDITION

Since 1952, when I wrote the foreword to the first
edition of this book, wonderful Elena has been very busy
indeed. Her frozen food business, which she runs with
the help of her two sons, Larry and Billy, is thriving.
She herself goes to the plant every day, tasting each new
batch of tamale filling or enchilada sauce, considering
and testing new Mexican foods to be added to the
growing list, taking telephone calls (it delights her that
new phone customers never suspect her blindness),
and adding her own special brand of happiness to the
entire business. She has also written two books since
this one. The first is *Elena's Secrets of Mexican Cooking*
(Prentice-Hall). The other book is called, simply,
Elena, and is the story of her incredible life. *Elena*,
though an autobiography, is quite naturally filled with
thoughts of food, for cooking is a very important
part of this endearing woman's life.

This book is a revised edition of the original, with the
addition of a few wanted recipes such as seviche and
tamales. It has been republished because of the many
requests for it. It seems that Elena's admirers—and
they are innumerable—feel that to own one of her books
is to want them all.

And so Elena goes merrily, busily on. As her fame increases more and more exciting things come her way. Recently, for instance, she went to New York to advise Restaurant Associates on the Mexican foods to be served at their fascinating new restaurant, La Fonda del Sol. She is constantly in demand as a speaker, for there is no one who can cheer and inspire an audience as can our darling Elena. Who could possibly stay gloomy while watching that quick smile and listening to that joyous voice? For Elena, though she has learned the hard way, is a truly happy woman as well as a superb cook.

HELEN EVANS BROWN

elena's fiesta recipes

appetizers,
tacos,
sandwiches

ABALONE COCKTAIL

I love to cook so much that I suspect my friends think I
spend hours over everything I make. They should see me
prepare this delicious cocktail of canned abalone from
Baja California, which can be found at any Mexican
food store or fancy grocery, as can the prepared
Jalapeña sauce I use. I simply dice the abalone meat,
add the juice, season all with lemon juice, and chill
thoroughly. At serving time I let my guests add
Jalapeña sauce to suit their individual tastes, as this
sauce is very hot.

Another of my quick cocktail tricks is to marinate
prawns or shrimps in a sauce made by mixing one part
of brown prepared mustard with two parts of French
dressing.

&❧ Elena speaks of abalones from Baja California
because California state law prohibits the exportation of
abalones, which is lucky for us Californians. Otherwise
every gourmet in the country would be importing
these succulent mollusks, leaving none for us.

3

MARINATED FISH COCKTAIL
₹☙ Seviche

Acapulco has contributed much to the fairly recent
popularity of this dish with North Americans, as it is
considered a regional dish of that beautiful city, although
seviche is served much throughout Mexico wherever
fresh fish is available. Although any firm-fleshed,
boneless, white fish will do, I am partial to red snapper
or pompano. Don't be horrified when you note the
fish is not cooked: it really *is*, not by heat, but by the
action of the lemon juice. There are many versions
of seviche, but I find the following combinations
particularly delicious. Fresh cilantro, sometimes called
Chinese parsley, is especially authentic and delightful
when it can be obtained. Otherwise oregano does nicely.

SEVICHE CON ALCAPARRAS (CAPERS):

1 lb. fresh white fish
¾ cup lemon juice
1 tsp. salt
Fresh gr. pepper
3 or 4 canned green chiles,
  seeded and chopped
2 medium tomatoes,
  skinned and cut up

1 large onion, chopped or
  sliced thin
2 or 3 tbs. capers
4 tbs. olive oil
2 tbs. dry white wine or
  vinegar
2 tsp. oregano or cilantro
Avocado for garnish

*Cut the fish, skinless, and boneless, into small pieces, and
place in porcelain dish. Cover with lemon or lime juice, salt
and pepper, and allow to marinate in refrigerator for several
hours. Add other ingredients, mix lightly, and chill further.
Serve very cold in shells or cocktail glasses garnished with
sliced avocado. This amount serves 6 or 8.*

SEVICHE CON ACEITUNAS (OLIVES):

*Proceed as above, omitting capers and green chiles and
substituting 12 to 16 sliced green stuffed olives and one*

4

*avocado, cut up and added instead of used for garnish, and
fresh cilantro to taste. This is very mild, but delicious. It can be
pepped up by the addition of a little Jalapeña sauce.
Serves 6 or 8.*

ষ্ণ Seviche is versatility itself! On a recent prowl
around restaurants throughout Mexico, we found seviche
as variable as it was ubiquitous. Sometimes shrimps,
clams, or oysters were used. All were different, some
better than others, but all surprisingly good. Experiment
with your own combinations. We have had great
success with fresh halibut.

PICKLED WAX PEPPERS

ষ্ণ *Chiles Curtidos*

These hot little peppers are perfect to serve with meats,
or as an accompaniment to cocktails, as you would
serve olives. I put them up in pint jars much like
cucumber pickles. After filling the jars with the washed
chiles which have been pricked with a fork, I add
to each jar 1 or 2 peeled cloves of garlic, sliced onions,
½ teaspoon of salt, ½ teaspoon of oregano, and then
I fill the jar with vinegar. Be sure to add more vinegar
as needed to keep the chiles covered, as they absorb
it after a few days.

ষ্ণ Lucky Peter Piper picked his peck of peppers
already pickled, but this method is almost as simple.

TACOS

Tacos are Mexican sandwiches—tortillas with filling
rolled or folded inside, then fried, toasted, or baked.

Many people don't think of tacos as a party dish, but they certainly are, particularly when served with guacamole or mantequilla de pobre (pp. 12-14). Shredded lettuce is served only on the fried taco, which of course must be opened for this addition after frying, then sprinkled with grated cheese and a spoonful of tomato sauce (given below). You really have to pick these up with your fingers. For fried or baked tacos the machine-made tortillas are better, because they are thinner and don't absorb as much fat, but if your tortillas are more than a day old, be careful to heat them before rolling to prevent cracking. Before heating dampen the underside of the tortilla (never the face!) with the moistened palm of the hand and never heat the face side first. The face side is the side that is peeled off to make raspadas. Always roll tacos with the filling on the face.

Toasted tacos are made like a turnover, folded edge to edge and toasted right on the gas flame, grill, or electrical unit. I butter the inside first, regardless of filling, and I butter the *outside!* The most popular toasted taco is the quesadilla (p. 10). Made over an outside grill these are ideal for picnics or patio parties.

Baked tacos are not as common in Mexico as the others, but I like them particularly because they make entertaining so much easier. They can be made ahead for a large crowd and baked for half an hour before serving. I have made baked tacos for as many as 150 guests. Simply fry tortillas lightly, stuff, roll, and arrange in a long baking pan. Pour tomato sauce or sour cream over the top, sprinkle with grated cheese, and bake in a 350° oven. Taco fillings may be as varied as those for sandwiches. Here are a few suggestions:

6

Tacos de Chorizo: Fry chorizo (p. 92) with chopped onion.

Tacos de Frijol: Refry beans (p. 38), add pieces of your favorite cheese and chile sauce. Roll and bake or fry.

Tacos de Carne: Use any leftover meats and vegetables, chopped coarsely, add a little chile sauce, roll, and fry.

Tacos de Queso: These are better known as quesadillas. Butter tortillas on both sides, place a piece of melting cheese on face side, fold like a turnover, and toast on griddle.

Tacos de Sardina: Combine skinned, chopped tomato, minced onion, sardines in oil, vinegar, a bit of crushed oregano, and chopped green chile (optional). Fill tortillas, roll, and fry. If sardines in tomato sauce are used, add a little grated cheese.

Tomato Sauce for Tacos: Add minced onion to skinned chopped fresh tomatoes or tomato sauce. Season with salt and pepper and chopped green chiles or Jalapeña sauce to taste.

&ᴥ Don't let the tortilla "face" business throw you. If Elena can tell the face by feeling, you can certainly do so by looking. It's the thin side that is slightly raised, like a blister.

Easy Tacos for Teenagers: In the West and Southwest, tacos are nudging hamburgers out of first place in popularity with the hungry teenage set, and why not? They make a perfect informal party dish for young *or* old, and everyone can join in the fun of preparation. I give here a very simple Americanized recipe for two dozen tacos. How many this will serve depends, of course, on individual capacities.

24 tortillas   Oil for frying

FILLING

1 large onion, chopped   1 tbs. chile pepper
2½ lbs. ground beef   (or more)
2 cloves garlic, mashed   ½ tsp. ground comino
Salt and pepper to taste   ½ tsp. ground coriander
2 medium tomatoes, peeled   1 tsp. dried oregano
   and chopped

GARNISH

1 large head lettuce, chopped   1 large onion, chopped
1 lb. Cheddar or Monterey   1 bottle Taco sauce
   Jack cheese, shredded

   Combine chopped onion and garlic with meat in large frying
pan. No oil is needed unless meat is very lean. Cook until
meat is brown, breaking it up with a fork as it cooks;
then add tomatoes and seasonings and simmer to blend.
Meanwhile, set up a production line. While the host cooks the
meat filling, let one guest chop onions, others shred lettuce
and cheese. A fourth can fry the tortillas lightly in about ¾
inch oil, then wrap each in a paper napkin and fold
through the center to hold the filling. First add meat,
then grated cheese (the heat of the meat will melt it), chopped
onions, lettuce, and finally a douse of Taco sauce to suit
individual taste.

TORTILLA SNACKS

For these little snacks, much like tacos, I trim off the
border of the tortillas with scissors before heating or
frying them, as it makes them a little easier to eat.

DEVILED TORTILLA ROLLS

12 tortillas   Oil for frying
1 can deviled ham   Guacamole (p. 12) to cover

8

*Heat trimmed tortillas over stove, spread with ham, roll,
and secure with toothpicks. Fry in oil and serve hot,
covered with guacamole.*

FANCY TORTILLA ROLLS

12 tortillas
¼ lb. boiled ham
½ lb. any yellow cheese
2 medium-sized tomatoes,
    peeled and chopped
Green chiles, chopped, to taste

Salt to taste
1 tbs. minced parsley
1 tbs. finely chopped onion
Oil to fry
Guacamole to cover tortillas

*Chop ham coarsely, and cut cheese in small cubes. Add
tomatoes, chiles, salt, parsley, onion. Spread on tortillas, roll,
secure with toothpicks, fry, and serve hot, covered with
guacamole.*

CHEESE TORTILLA ROLLS

12 tortillas
3 tbs. oil
1 tbs. chopped onion
2 medium-sized peeled
    tomatoes

2 peeled green chiles, chopped
Salt to taste
½ lbs. Monterey Jack cheese
1 cup sour cream

*In 1 tablespoon of oil fry the chopped onion, tomatoes, and
chiles. Add salt. In remaining oil fry the tortillas lightly
until just soft. On each tortilla place a slice of cheese and
then roll. Place rolled tortillas on platter, cover with tomato
mixture and sour cream. Let heat in oven until cheese
melts before serving.*

ঌ Different and hearty, these would be magnificent
to serve at those cocktail parties where the guests
linger and linger.

STUFFED FRESH CORN MEAL TURNOVERS
ঌ *Molotes*

Other shortening may be used here in place of the lard,
but it will not have the distinctive flavor the lard

gives. An American probably would not detect the
difference, but a Mexican would.

TORTILLA MIXTURE

½ cup lard	1 lb. masa (found at Mexican
1 tsp. salt	stores)

SUGGESTED FILLINGS

Refried beans (p. 38)	d. Brains, cooked and seasoned.
with fried chorizo.	e. Any leftover chopped meat.
b. Any good melting cheese.	f. Picadillo (fancy hash)
c. Strips of green, peeled chiles.	(p. 64).

*Beat lard until light and creamy, add masa and salt,
divide into 12 balls and pat out between the palms of the
hands until the size of a saucer. Spread on filling, fold as a
turnover, pressing edges together, and fry in deep fat
until golden brown. Serve hot.*

ટે For a test of real Spartan self-control try limiting
yourself to *one* of these. On second thought, don't.
Life is too short and these are too tantilizing.

MEXICAN FRIED TURNOVERS
ટે *Quesadillas Fritas*

These are marvelous to serve with cocktails. They also
make a magnificent accompaniment to salads for a
complete light meal. Masa can be found at Mexican food
stores almost everywhere. Make small tortillas of it
and fill with any combination you wish. Quesadillas can
be made in advance and fried at the last minute
before serving.

TORTILLA MIXTURE

½ cup shortening or lard	½ cup flour
1 ½ lbs. masa	1 tsp. salt

10

SUGGESTED FILLINGS

a. Chorizo (Mexican sausage), removed from casing, crumbled, fried without added oil, then scrambled with eggs.

b. Strips of Monterey Jack or Cheddar cheese with strips of green peeled chiles.

c. Seasoned, chopped leftover meats or refried beans (p. 38) with cheese.

Beat the shortening until light and creamy, mix with masa, flour, and salt, and form into balls the size of a walnut. Pat out each between the palms of the hands, making a small tortilla. Spreal filling on tortilla, but not clear to the edge, fold over, pinch edges together, and fry in deep hot oil until golden. Drain on absorbent paper and serve hot. This amount should make about 24 turnovers.

Elena's quick, skillful little hands fairly fly as she pats these out. Suggestion of a rolling pin will probably bring forth one of her favorite remarks, laughingly:

"*Para tonto, no se estudia.*"
"You don't have to study to be dumb."

LITTLE MEXICAN TURNOVERS

Empanaditas

Empanadas for appetizers should be made very small, about as big around as the top of a whiskey glass. They are just a mouthful. If you wish to deep-fat fry these rather than bake them, be sure to cut your shortening to ½ cup. Empanaditas are wonderful to have around for the holidays.

2 cups flour
1 tsp. salt
⅔ cup lard (and I mean lard)
Ice water (just enough to blend pastry)

Make a rich pastry dough of the above, roll out, and cut into tiny rounds. (I always chill my dough before rolling.) Place a spoonful of any desired filling on one-half, dampen edge, fold over, and press edges together. Bake in a 375° oven for 15 to 20 minutes, or deep-fat-fry until golden. For fillings try anchovy paste, deviled ham, grated cheese mixed with butter, creamed chicken or tuna, or picadillo (p. 64).

ે Once you try these beguiling little morsels for cocktails, you will find yourself encasing everything in the larder. Let your imagination run wild.

GUACAMOLE

Guacamole has become best known to Americans, perhaps, as a cocktail spread or "dunk," but it is also a salad, a sauce, a filling for tortillas, or a garnish. Mexicans do not mash their guacamole to a smooth paste as do Americans—there are lumps in it. Occasionally try the addition of crumbled bacon, chopped peanuts, or best of all, chicharrones (crisp fried bacon rinds, sometimes called cracklings).

1 large tomato, peeled	*2 tbs. vinegar or 1 tbs. lemon*
1 small onion, minced	*juice*
Chopped green chile to taste	*Salt to taste*
(Jalapeña sauce may be	*2 avocados, mashed*
used)	

Chop the peeled tomato very fine with the minced onion. Add the vinegar, chile, and seasoning and let stand until ready to serve; then add the mashed avocado, which will turn dark if allowed to stand too long.

ે There are probably as many versions of this Mexican classic as there are cooks, but we have always

felt that the addition of mayonnaise was carrying
coals to Newcastle, as avocado is loaded with its own oil.

LITTLE MEATS
ठ✍ *Carnitas*

I first came across these delicious little meat cubes many
years ago at one of those little food stands (puestos)
in the dinky little town of Siete Cumbres on the way to
Puebla. They were served with tostadas (crisp fried
pieces of raspadas) and poor man's butter (see below).
Carnitas make a wonderful buffet supper dish,
or a good taco filling, too.

2 lbs. lean pork	½ tsp. Ac'cent
(boneless butt)	Salt and pepper to taste

*Cut the pork in 1-inch cubes, sprinkle with Ac'cent, salt,
and pepper, and let stand for 1 hour or so. Place in a
shallow baking pan in 300° oven for about 2 hours, pouring
off the fat as it accumulates. Serve hot to eight persons.*

ठ✍ Just watch the men go for these! They have all
the charm of spareribs without so much as one telltale
bone to be counted against the cocktail guest. Here
is one of Elena's most exciting contributions to
North-of-the-Border cuisine—nuggets of crisp, juicy
pork, simply flavored with all the natural goodness
of the meat.

POOR MAN'S BUTTER
ठ✍ *Mantequilla de Pobre*

This is almost like guacamole, except that it is not as
smooth and has no onion. In Mexico, mantequilla

13

de pobre is served as a sauce over any gravyless meat or chicken. It is a delicious accompaniment to the carnitas above.

2 *large tomatoes, peeled*	1 *tbs. salad oil*
2 *medium-sized avocados*	¼ *tsp. Ac'cent*
3 *tbs. red wine vinegar*	*Salt to taste*

Cut tomatoes and acovados into small cubes, add vinegar, oil, Ac'cent, and salt. Toss gently until well mixed. Let stand at room temperature for about 30 minutes before serving.

ϡ Poor man's butter indeed! Not for unfortunates who must harvest their avocados at the local market. But who minds a few cents?—this is fit for royalty.

EASY TEA CAKES

Here are two lazy but delicious suggestions to serve with a cup of tea or coffee.

a. Cut raisin bread with a doughnut cutter. Butter and cover with cinnamon and sugar. Brown under broiler just until sugar melts.

b. Toast slices of pound cake. Spread with butter, cinnamon, and sugar while still warm.

THREE-DECKER MEXICAN HAMBURGERS

Cut hamburger roll in three slices. Chop green peeled chiles and mix with chopped pickle relish and chopped peanuts for bottom of the bun. Cover with a well-seasoned cooked hamburger cake. Add middle slice of roll. Spread with mayonnaise, top with tomato slice and third slice of bun. When making these for children you will probably want to omit the chiles.

soups

DRY SOUP WITH MUSHROOMS
𐅀❞ *Sopa Seca con Hongos*

In Mexico, on festive occasions, it is customary to serve
not one but two soups. The dry soup is brought on
right after the liquid one and is a separate course in
itself. These dry soups are generally made of rice or one
of the small pastes such as vermicelli, simmered in
broth until all the liquid is absorbed.

½ cup salad oil	*½ lb. fresh sautéed mushrooms*
½ lb. vermicelli	*2 cups chicken broth*
1 tbs. minced onion	*½ tsp. Ac'cent*
¾ cup canned tomatoes	*Salt to taste*
1 (4-oz.) can mushroom	*1 cup coarsely shredded*
stems and pieces, or	*Cheddar cheese*

*Heat the oil in a large, heavy skillet. Add uncooked
vermicelli and sauté until golden brown, stirring gently
with a fork while cooking to prevent its becoming too dark.
Remove the vermicelli to a 2-quart casserole, pouring off all
but 2 tablespoons of oil from the skillet. Add the minced
onion to this oil and cook until golden, then add the
tomatoes, mushrooms (including liquid), chicken broth, and
seasonings. Heat all to boiling and pour over vermicelli.
Cover tightly and bake in a 300° oven for 45 minutes.
Sprinkle cheese over the top and continue baking,
uncovered, 15 minutes longer. Serves eight.*

15

ॐ Should you not feel quite up to getting away with *two* nourishing soups before your main meal, may we suggest this as a fine substantial luncheon or supper dish?

TORTILLA BALL SOUP
ॐ *Sopa de Albóndigas de Tortilla*

You will notice that almost all the Mexican soups given here are just good rich broth with some sort of little balls added for both interest and flavor. The Breakfast cheese called for in this recipe can usually be found at an Italian delicatessen, but Brie may be substituted, in which case it is simply mixed with the ground tortillas and not ground with them.

6 leftover tortillas *1 egg*
½ lb. Breakfast cheese *Salt and pepper to taste*
1 tbs. butter

Soak the tortillas in water, drain, and grind with the cheese. Add melted butter, egg, and seasoning. Make into small balls the size of a Bing cherry and fry until brown. Add these to any broth, with more grated cheese if desired.

ॐ If you don't happen to have any leftover tortillas around, rather than miss this, we recommend letting some brand-new ones languish a couple of days.

FISHBALL SOUP
ॐ *Sopa de Albóndigas de Pescado*

When making this soup ask your butcher or fish dealer for a fish head and trimmings for the broth. I buy halibut for the fishballs, but any mild-flavored white fish will do.

16

SOUP

1 fish head and trimmings	1 bay leaf
3 qts. water	Salt and pepper to taste
1 large onion	1/4 cup tomato puree
2 garlic cloves	2 large potatoes, peeled
1 tbs. oregano	and cubed
8 peppercorns	

FISHBALLS

1 1/2 lbs. white fish	1 tsp. oregano
2 beaten eggs	Salt and pepper

Simmer the fish trimmings, onion, garlic, and seasonings in water until a rich broth is made. Strain. Cook the diced potatoes with the tomato puree in a little oil for 5 minutes and add to the broth. Simmer while making the fishballs by grinding the boned, raw halibut, adding beaten eggs and seasonings, then rolling into little balls about the size of a walnut. Drop these into the boiling broth, cover tightly and cook for 30 minutes. This will serve six to eight.

ào No matter your chowder school of thought, be it Manhattan or New England, forget it over a steamy bowl of this marvelous marine concoction.

SOUP, ACAPULCO STYLE

The beautiful little town of Taxco initiated me to this delightful soup, named for another lovely place. Masa, which I discuss on p. 86, is used here to make the noodle-like strips which go into the broth.

MASA STRIPS

1/2 lb. masa	1/2 tsp. salt
1/2 tsp. chile powder	1/2 tsp. baking powder

BROTH

2 tbs. oil	2 qts. beef or chicken broth
1 (8-oz.) can tomato sauce	

Mix all the dry ingredients with the masa, make into balls the size of walnuts and pat between the palms of the hands into thin pancakes. (A rolling pin, if you must!) Cut these pancakes into thin strips about ½ inch wide, allow to dry an hour or so as you would noodles, then fry in plenty of oil until brown. For the broth, heat the oil, add the tomato sauce and allow to cook for a few minutes, then add the broth, cover, and simmer. At serving time add the fried masa strips to the broth, and sprinkle grated cheese over the top. Serves eight.

驴 Try this soup. It should enjoy the popularity of its famous namesake. Elena, with her nimble little hands, hasn't much sympathy for awkward gringos, like us, who occasionally resort to the rolling pin.

ELENA'S ITALIAN SOUP
驴 *Sopa Romana*

I make little meat-filled ravioli for this, usually with chicken, as given here. When I use beef stock instead of chicken, I substitute chopped beef for the chicken in the filling, and omit the nutmeg. I know you may be thinking that all this sounds tedious, but there is nothing difficult about it, and believe me, it is well worth a little effort.

NOODLE DOUGH

1 cup sifted flour	*1 beaten egg*
½ tsp. salt	*1 tsp. water*

FILLING

1 cup cooked chicken, finely chopped	*1 whole egg*
	1 egg yolk
2 tbs. butter	*Pinch of nutmeg*
2 tbs. grated Parmesan cheese	*Salt and pepper to taste*

18

Make a stiff dough of the noodle ingredients, turn out on
a lightly floured board and knead gently, just enough to
smooth out the dough. Let stand about 5 minutes to
"loosen," then roll out very thin and cut into 2-inch rounds.
(This should make about 24 of these.) For the filling,
simply cook the chicken in butter until lightly browned,
add cheese, seasonings, and the egg and egg yolk beaten
together. Place a small spoonful of the filling in the center
of each, moisten edges, and fold over, sealing together.
Drop these, a few at a time so that boiling is not retarded,
into 1½ to 2 quarts of well-seasoned, boiling chicken broth.
Cover and simmer until tender (about 30 minutes).
Grated Parmesan cheese should be sprinkled over the
top of this soup. Serves six.

ૄ⃥ What a prologue for a happy meal! Elena pats
her round little tummy when she speaks of this,
and we share her enthusiasm.

MEXICAN POTATO BALL SOUP
ૄ⃥ *Sopa de Bolitas de Papa*

These are the same potato balls which make such a
delicious vegetable, only much smaller and
shallow-fried rather than deep-fried.

3 *medium-sized baked*	2 *eggs*
potatoes	2 *tsp. grated Parmesan*
½ *cup water*	*cheese*
2 *tbs. butter*	1 *tbs. finely chopped parsley*
½ *cup flour*	*Salt and pepper to taste*

Scoop potatoes out of shells while hot, and mash smooth.
Measure out 2 cups of potatoes, loosely packed, and to these
add this batter: Boil the water with butter, add flour all
at once, and mix well until it separates from the side of the
pan. Add the unbeaten eggs, one at a time, beating well,

19

then the grated cheese, parsley, and seasoning. Shape into
small balls, roll in flour, and fry in butter. Drop these
into hot broth just before serving.

8◆ Tiny potato cream puffs, and as delightful here
in miniature as in the full-sized version to
complement your roast.

SOUP WITH MASA TURNOVERS
8◆ *Sopa de Quesadillas*

Quesadillas are little turnovers, made from masa, and
fried. I give the recipe for them on p. 10. Make them
this same way for soup, only smaller. Brush each round
with melted butter and sprinkle generously with
grated cheese before folding over and sealing the edges.
Fry in deep fat until golden, and place several in
each soup plate before filling with well-seasoned broth.
Finely chopped hard-cooked egg sprinkled over the
soup is a nice touch, I think.

8◆ *"Metiendo muchas cucharas, echan a perder*
el caldo."
"Too many cooks spoil the broth."

ITALIAN MARRIAGE SOUP
8◆ *Maritata*

An Italian friend gave me the recipe for this soup,
which as its name implies, is served traditionally at the
marriage feast. It certainly belongs in a "fiesta" book.

4 cups rich chicken broth   *1 cup cream*
   (seasoned)   *2 egg yolks, beaten*
⅓ cup pastina   *Grated Parmesan cheese*

20

Cook pastina in the boiling broth for a few minutes, stirring now and then. Add cream and simmer gently. Just before serving add beaten egg yolks to soup. Sprinkle grated Parmesan on the bottom of the soup plates or tureen, pour in the hot soup, and serve quickly.

ৡ▰ An old Italian custom—and a wise one. A bowl of this soul-satisfying soup should get any new marriage off to a fine start, and enrich many an old one.

"En el amor, el estómago siempre vence al corazón."
"In love, the stomach always conquers the heart."

SOUR CREAM SOUP
ৡ▰ *Minguiche*

"Ahora es cuando, chile verde, le has de dar sabor al caldo."
"Now is the time, green chile, for you to season the broth."

During the season of Lent this soup is very popular in the state of Jalisco. The name "minguiche" usually means a combination of sour cream, chile, and cheese.

1 tbs. butter	*1 qt. sour cream*
1 medium-sized onion, cut in rings	*¼ cup milk*
	Salt and pepper to taste
1 long green chile or ½ bell pepper, diced	*¼ lb. Monterey Jack cheese, cubed, or Breakfast cheese*

Melt butter and cook onion rings and chile or pepper until tender, about 10 minutes. Add sour cream and milk, season, and heat thoroughly. A few minutes before serving add the cheese cubes.

ৡ▰ An unusual soup—unusually good. *"Jalisco Nunca Pierde!"* Hurray for Jalisco!

HEARTY SPANISH SOUP
ɕ✀ Cocido

The difference between a cocido and a sopa is that the
cocido is practically a meal in itself. All this needs
is the addition of garlic French bread and a dessert.
Garbanzos may be added here. The typical cocido with
garbanzos is, of course, the famous Spanish puchero,
a recipe which appears in my other cook book.

2 lbs. beef shanks	3 zucchini, sliced
3 qts. water	½ lb. green beans, cut up
2 cloves of garlic	Salt to taste
1 onion, sliced	3 ears of corn (fresh or frozen)
8 peppercorns	cut into 1-inch pieces
3 carrots, sliced	

*Start the meat in cold water. Make a rich broth by
cooking it slowly with garlic, onion, pepper, and salt. When
the meat is tender, strain off the broth, add the vegetables,
corn last, and cook slowly until done. Add the meat, cut
in cubes, to the soup. If extra piquancy is desired, you
may serve this with Jalapeña sauce.*

ɕ✀ A Spanish version of Brunswick stew. Pick the
corn up in your fingers. Elena says the corncobs give
the stew its wonderful flavor.

salads

CHRISTMAS EVE SALAD
ใ๏ *Ensalada de Noche Buena*

This salad is a Mexican holiday tradition. I have
changed it slightly the better to suit my American
taste and yours. In Mexico shredded lettuce is used, as
is the jícama, a fruit rather tasteless in itself which
assimilates other flavors. You probably couldn't find a
jícama anyway, so why bother? Mexicans usually put
just sugar on the salad, but I think you will like it
better accompanied by a bowl of mayonnaise thinned
with the fruit juices and a little cream.

*Equal quantities of the following, depending on how many
are to be served:*

Beets, cooked and sliced	*Unsalted peanuts*
Pineapple chunks, fresh	*Pomegranate seeds (dig*
or frozen	*them out)*
Apples, cored and sliced	*Mayonnaise thinned with fruit*
Orange sections, peeled	*juices and a little cream*
Bananas, sliced	
Jícama, sliced thin	

*Arrange all the fruits as attractively as you can in a
large glass bowl or platter (Mexican glass, if you have it).
Sprinkle peanuts over all; then pomegranate seeds. Serve
dressing over the salad or separately.*

23

᠍᠍ A fiesta recipe to be treasured, this beautiful classic of Mexican cuisine might well become a holiday tradition in your home. For the annual tree-trimming party, perhaps, followed or preceded by steaming bowls of oyster stew.

AVOCADO AND ORANGE SALAD

3 avocados   Lettuce
2 oranges   Fresh mint for garnish
French dressing

Halve the avocados and scoop out the pulp with a French ball cutter, saving the shells. Peel the oranges, cut into pieces, and combine with avocado. Marinate in French dressing for about ½ hour. Fill the avocado shells with the avocado and orange. Serve on lettuce, garnished with leaves of fresh mint. Serves six.

Another good avocado salad is made by dicing the avocado, combining with water cress, and serving with French dressing.

GREEN OR RED FRESH PEPPERS

᠍᠍ *Pimientos Frescos Verdes o Colorados*

Buy fresh green or red bell peppers for this. The green ones are, of course, almost always available, but the gorgeous flame-red peppers are usually limited to the early fall season.

Place fresh peppers under the broiler flame, turning, so that all sides are exposed to the direct heat. When the skin blisters all over, place them in a paper bag, close tightly, and allow to steam for about 20 minutes. You will find that the skin will peel off just like a glove. Remove seeds and stems, and cut peppers into strips. Rub a serving bowl

24

with garlic, add peppers, and cover with oil, vinegar, salt
and pepper to taste. Let these stand at least 2 hours
before using.

દે We believe this recipe title should read Green
and Red Peppers, as the two look so handsome together.

CELERY ROOT SALAD

Rather than peel the tough outside skin of celery root
before cooking, I simply scrub the roots, boil in water
with salt and lemon until tender, then plunge them
into cold water. The peeling comes off much more
readily this way. Immediately slice the celery root
into a bowl of French dressing and allow to marinate
for several hours. Serve on greens, crossing the
celery root with strips of anchovies.

TORPEDO ONION SALAD

Torpedo onions are the long red variety. Simply slice
them in rings and allow to stand in 1 cup of ice
water with salt for an hour or so, then drain and
marinate with French dressing.

ARTICHOKES IN MUSTARD SAUCE

"*Más vale un pájaro en mano que cien volando.*"
"A bird in the hand is better than a hundred flying."

If you cannot buy fresh baby artichokes, canned
artichoke hearts may be used here, but are not nearly
so good.

12 baby artichokes　　　　　*French dressing*
Brown prepared mustard

*Remove first few leaves from artichokes, clip points,
and cook in boiling salted water with a garlic clove and*

*½ lemon, sliced. When tender, drain well, turning upside
down. Make mustard sauce by combining one part brown
prepared mustard with two parts French dressing. Marinate
artichokes for several hours in this sauce, turning
until thoroughly soaked.*

ટ Simple, isn't it? Yet so impressive, and so good!

EGGPLANT SALAD

2 eggplants   *½ cup chopped celery*
Lemon juice   *¼ cup French dressing*
1 clove garlic   *Romaine lettuce*
Salt to taste   *Mayonnaise*
¼ cup minced onion

*Peel the eggplant and then dice it. Drop into boiling
salted water to which a clove of garlic and a little lemon
juice have been added. Cook eggplant until just barely
tender, taking care that it does not become mushy. Drain
and mix with onion, celery and French dressing. Turn out
in bowl lined with romaine and serve with mayonnaise.
Serves six or eight.*

ELENA'S POTATO SALAD

*Cook in their jackets as many potatoes as are desired.
Peel, slice into rings, and marinate in oil and vinegar, just
enough to coat the potatoes. Add salt and pepper and grated
onion according to taste, and let stand for several hours.
Just before serving, whip some cream and add to the
potatoes. Last, mix in mayonnaise to suit, minced parsley,
and chopped pimientos.*

ટ Elena says that you may add chopped pickles
and/or hard-cooked eggs, but to us it would be a
desecration, like drawing a mustache on the Mona
Lisa. But suit yourself.

POTATO AND SARDINE SALAD

4 cups cooked potatoes, sliced
12 small pickled onions
3 fresh tomatoes
1 can sardines in oil
3 hard-cooked eggs
2 tbs. finely minced parsley

3 dill pickles
1/4 cup oil, including oil
  from sardines
1/3 cup vinegar
Salt and pepper to taste

Place sliced potatoes on large platter and sprinkle with pickled onions cut in half. Slice tomatoes over potatoes, then add sardines, broken up with a fork, and rings of hard-cooked eggs. Sprinkle parsley over the top, and slice dill pickles in rings around the platter. Rub a bowl with garlic, add oil, vinegar, salt and pepper, and allow to stand for 15 minutes before pouring over top of salad. Let the whole thing remain in the refrigerator for a half hour before serving time.

ও Some sticky, sultry summer night this, with a bowl of soup, would make supper.

CAULIFLOWER AND AVOCADO SALAD

A very Mexican combination, and nice to serve with Mexican food as a cold vegetable. It's mighty pretty as a salad. As a matter of fact, for luncheons it will double as a centerpiece when gaily decorated. My friends tell me it looks like a Mexican hat. Here's how to do it:

1 large head cooked
  cauliflower
3 tbs. wine vinegar or
  lemon juice
6 tbs. oil
Salt and pepper
1/2 cup blanched ground
  almonds

3 very ripe avocados, mashed
1 small onion, minced
Dash of nutmeg
Lettuce
Radish rosettes
Cucumber and tomato slices
Stuffed green olives

*Place cooked cauliflower in a deep dish and pour over it
the oil, vinegar, salt and pepper. Chill for several hours.
Mash the avocados with almonds, onion, salt and nutmeg,
adding 3 tablespoons of the vinegar-oil marinade used for
the cauliflower.*

*Center the cauliflower on large chop plate and ice it with
avocado mixture. Stick toothpicks into radish rosettes. Now
poke them into the top of cauliflower in the form of a cross
or some other pattern of your choice. Around the base
(or brim!) arrange alternate rows of cucumber slices and
tomato slices, extending them from the cauliflower nearly to
the edge of the plate. For a final flourish, spear stuffed
green olives on toothpicks (two or three per stick)
and anchor them in cucumber slices, one to a row. Result:
An edible sombrero.*

ह‍ Here is a supremely delightful dish guaranteed
to get you nothing but compliments.

PIMIENTO BEEF SALAD

"Tengo una hambre que parece dos."
"I'm so hungry, I feel like twins."

6 slices leftover cooked beef	*1 head lettuce, shredded*
1 can red pimientos, diced	*French dressing*
½ cup green olives, cut	*Red onion slices for garnish*
from pits	

*Cut beef into long, narrow strips. Marinate in French
dressing for an hour. Then toss with diced pimientos, olives,
and shredded lettuce. Garnish with rings of red onion.
Serves six.*

ह‍ A fine al fresco luncheon salad, if you are lucky
enough to have any leftover beef these days. Sliced
cooked tongue or corned beef should taste good
here, too.

MOLDED CHERRY SALAD WITH SHERRY

I like to serve this salad for buffet suppers, as it looks beautiful and is delicious. It may be made in a ring mold, filling the center with melon balls and garnishing with mint leaves. Other times I use a fish mold, placing a maraschino cherry for the eye, and decorating the fish with a pastry bag filled with a mixture of soft cream cheese and a little mayonnaise. I turn the fish out on a large platter and garnish with pears, peaches, or apricots.

2 packages cream cheese
1 No. 2 can bing cherries, pitted
2 packages cherry-flavored
   gelatin

2 cups boiling water
1 cup Sherry wine
1 cup cherry juice

Chill the cream cheese. Form into miniature balls and stuff into pitted cherries. Arrange stuffed cherries in bottom of fancy mold. Dissolve gelatin in boiling water. Add Sherry and cherry juice. Pour over cherries and chill until firm.

COLD STUFFED CARROTS

ह्ళ *Zanahorias Frías Rellenas con Sardina*

A Spanish woman from Andalusia gave me this divine recipe. It may be prepared with cold medium-sized potatoes instead of the carrots. Either version makes a hearty main-dish salad.

12 large carrots
1 can large sardines in
   tomato sauce
4 hard-cooked eggs
¼ lb. blanched ground almonds

½ cup oil
1 tbs. wine vinegar
Salt and pepper to taste
2 tbs. minced parsley

29

*Boil the carrots until just barely tender, cut in half
lengthwise, and carefully scoop out the centers. Bone the
sardines and mash with the carrot centers, then refill
carrots, place on platter and chill thoroughly. Mix the
ground almonds with the mashed yolks of eggs, oil, vinegar,
salt and pepper. Cover the chilled carrots with this
mixture and garnish with minced parsley and chopped
whites of eggs.*

ह≫ The supreme glorification of the carrot! For a
festive and different luncheon serve this with Elena's
dry soup with mushrooms.

SARDINE-STUFFED ZUCCHINI

This is really more of a cold entrée than a salad.

12 medium-sized zucchini	*Salt, pepper, thyme, oregano*
1 large can sardines in	*to taste*
tomato sauce	*2 medium-sized avocados,*
1 large onion, sliced	*sliced*
4 large tomatoes	*Grated cheese*
2 tbs. wine vinegar	

*Cook zucchini just barely tender in salted water. Cut each
in half lengthwise and scoop out centers. Bone the sardines,
mince fine with centers of zucchini, and fill zucchini shells
with this mixture. Place filled zucchini on serving platter.
Peel and mash the tomatoes, seasoning with salt, pepper,
thyme, and oregano. Add vinegar and mix. Pour this sauce
over the zucchini and garnish with sliced onion, sliced
avocados, and grated cheese.*

ह≫ What a wonderful first course to pass around at
a barbecue while guests are drooling over those
tantalizing broiling smells!

EGGS

RANCH EGGS, CALIFORNIA STYLE
ᘒ Huevos Rancheros Californianos

Here is my adaptation of huevos rancheros to the taste of my California friends. In Mexico this dish would be served for breakfast, but if it seems too robust for that, try it for luncheon or supper. Hot garlic bread is good with this as, of course, are tortillas. The peeled green chiles can be replaced by a chile tepín here.

2 tbs. bacon drippings	1 No. 2 can solid pack tomatoes
2 tbs. minced onion	1/4 lb. sharp Cheddar cheese
1 can green peeled chiles, chopped (or to suit taste)	6 eggs
	Salt to taste

Fry onion in bacon drippings, add chile and tomatoes and let simmer until almost dry. Add cheese in cubes, and when almost melted drop in whole eggs, one at a time, cooking until desired consistency. Serve 2 eggs each to 3 hungry people.

ᘒ As is so true with many of Elena's recipes, just reading ingredients here gives you no idea how surprisingly magnificent these eggs are. Tasting is believing, and a treat. Be sure to use a very sharp cheese. For those of you really "in the know" about Mexican food, a side dish of nopalitos (cactus) goes very well with this. Frijoles, too, of course.

MEXICAN POACHED EGGS WITH CHEESE

 ஃ *Huevos en Salsa con Queso*

Frijoles refritos (Mexican fried beans) and tortillas are perfect accompaniments to this dish.

3 bell peppers	*1 tsp. oregano*
½ cup oil	*Salt and pepper to taste*
1 large onion, minced	*12 eggs*
2 cups tomato puree	*½ lb. Monterey Jack*
1 cup broth or consomme	*cheese, cubed*
1 tbs. minced parsley	

First skin the peppers by blistering them on all sides under the broiler, then steaming them for 15 minutes in a tightly closed paper bag. Peel, remove seeds, and cut in strips. In hot oil brown onion, add peppers, tomato puree, broth, and parsley. Season to taste, rubbing oregano between palms of hands. Simmer sauce for 15 minutes, then break eggs carefully and poach in sauce, adding one piece of cheese for each egg. Serves six.

ஃ A feast for Sunday breakfast after a late night! Reminiscent of huevos rancheros, these eggs should bring you fame.

EGGS IN MOLE SAUCE

ஃ *Huevos en Mole*

Mole is the classical sauce of Mexico, and is served with many dishes, as it is so popular, but chiefly over chicken and turkey. I give a recipe for mole sauce in my other book. Though not difficult to make, it has many, many ingredients and takes a little time. Since canned mole sauce is available at any Mexican store and many grocery stores, why bother?

1 can Mole Poblano	*Salt to taste*
1½ cups beef stock	*6 eggs*
3 tbs. oil	

Dilute mole with stock. Heat oil, add diluted sauce, salt to taste, and when sauce is boiling, break eggs into it, cover pan, and poach until firm. These eggs should be served with tortillas.

ठ✎ We almost had to twist Elena's arm to get this recipe in here, as she feels that "American people just don't like mole." So please don't let us down. We admit this miraculous sauce may seem a bit alarming at first, with its multiple ingredients (everything from chile to chocolate!), but give it a try. Like us, you may become an addict.

Mole Poblano is said to have originated at a convent in Puebla, when the nuns were thrown into a panic by an unexpected visit from the archbishop at a time when provisions were low and there was no wine to prepare the turkey. Reckless with desperation, the nuns ground up everything in the larder, and thus mole was born. It has become a national institution in Mexico.

ELEGANT STUFFED EGGS
ठ✎ *Huevos Rellenos "Elegancia"*

Probably every cook has a pet method for hard-cooking eggs. I have found that the eggs are always tender when added to boiling water (carefully!), then cooked for 10 minutes after water comes to second boil, and immediately put under cold water.

8 hard-cooked eggs	*Red chile sauce, p. 87*
¾ tsp. dry mustard	*1 bay leaf*
2 tbs. cream	*Sprig of thyme, or pinch of*
1 tsp. minced parsley	*dry thyme*
2 tbs. melted butter	*Sprig of sweet marjoram, or*
Salt and pepper to taste	*pinch of dry*

*Peel eggs and cut lengthwise. Remove yolks and mash well
with mustard, cream, parsley, butter, and salt and pepper
to taste. Stuff the eggs and press the two halves together.
Secure with toothpicks. Make red sauce, p. 87, omitting
chile powder, and adding bay leaf, thyme, and marjoram.
Simmer sauce for 20 minutes, remove herbs, and pour
over eggs. Serve these eggs in a nest of white rice or
noodles. With a green vegetable or salad, this is a
complete meal for four persons.*

ತ— Looking for something different for Easter
breakfast? Those elegant eggs cuddled in that rice nest
may give you an idea.

STUFFED EGGS, VALPARAISO STYLE
ತ— *Huevos Rellenos Valparaiso*

Here is a rather unusual recipe for stuffed eggs, as
these are deep-fried. This makes a wonderful luncheon
dish.

4 hard-cooked eggs	*¼ tsp. dry mustard*
Sufficient cream to make a	*½ tsp. Worcestershire sauce*
paste of egg yolks	*Pinch of paprika*
1 egg, beaten	*Salt to taste*
½ cup bread crumbs	*Deep fat for frying*

DEVIL SAUCE

1 tbs. butter	*½ cup dry Sherry*
1½ tbs. flour	*Salt and Cayenne pepper*
½ tsp. dry mustard	*to taste*
1 cup bouillon	

*Shell eggs, and cut in half lengthwise. Mash yolks with
cream and seasonings. Stuff whites and press halves
together again. Secure with toothpicks. Roll these in the
beaten egg and then in bread crumbs, then repeat. Fry in*

deep hot fat until golden brown. Drain on paper and serve
with devil sauce. To make sauce, melt butter, blend in flour,
add bouillon and Sherry; then add seasonings. Any of
the following may be added to the sauce: chopped parsley,
chives, olives, or mushrooms.

SCRAMBLED EGGS, MADRID STYLE
&⤳ *Huevos a la Madrileña*

This is a Spanish way with eggs and seems to call
for hot French garlic bread.

2 tbs. oil	*1 cup tomato puree*
⅓ cup raw ham, diced	*4 eggs*
2 tbs. minced onion	*Salt to taste*
1 clove of garlic, mashed	

*Fry diced ham in oil, add onion and garlic. Drain some of
the fat and add tomato puree. Season. Beat eggs and add,
stirring with a fork until set. Serves two.*

&⤳ If your esthetic senses rebel at eating pink
scrambled eggs, you might like to substitute a whole
peeled and chopped tomato here for the tomato puree.
Elena won't mind, as she often says:

"Cooks who won't vary a speck
  Give me a pain in the neck."

EGGS WITH TORTILLA
&⤳ *Huevos con Tortilla*

1 tortilla	*Grated cheese, or diced*
3 tbs. oil	*Monterey Jack or*
2 eggs	*Romano cheese*
Salt to taste	

35

With scissors cut the tortilla into eighths and fry in hot oil, not too crisp. Beat eggs, add salt, and pour over tortilla, turning as you would an omelet. Add cheese at end of cooking time, just long enough to melt. Serves one or two. (Probably only one!)

>> For the most irresistible scrambled eggs imaginable, try these on your A.M. or P.M. appetite. So simple, yet with a subtlety of flavor and texture beyond description.

SHIRRED EGGS IN SOUR CREAM WITH SPECIAL RICE

RICE

1 cup raw rice	2 cups water
3 tbs. butter	1 tsp. salt

EGGS

8 eggs	4 tbs. thick sour cream
2 tbs. butter	Salt and pepper to taste

Place rice in casserole. In separate pan, bring water to a boil with salt and butter, then pour over rice, cover, and cook for 45 minutes in 300° oven. Grease individual ramekins or custard cups with butter, and break 2 eggs into each. Season to taste, add 1 tablespoon of sour cream on each, and bake in a 350° oven until firm but not hard. Serves four.

EGGS WITH SAUSAGES

1 tbs. butter	2 tbs. grated Parmesan
¼ cup milk	cheese
4 eggs	Salt and pepper to taste
6 link sausages	

36

*Melt butter in heavy skillet, add milk, and allow to
simmer for a few minutes before breaking in the eggs. In
separate skillet place the sausages, add 1 tablespoon
of water, cover tightly, and cook for 5 minutes. Drain liquid
and brown sausages. This keeps sausages from shrinking.
Place browned sausages around eggs, sprinkle with
grated cheese, and place in 375° oven until eggs are
set. Serves two.*

ଛ Here is a comforting breakfast dish, designed to
tempt even the most jaded early morning appetite.

BANANA OMELET

There was a big question in my mind as to where I
should include this recipe. It may be a dessert, with
the additions I suggest here, or a delicious entrée when
served with fluffy steamed rice. However, it *is* an
omelet and hence printed here under Eggs.

6 eggs, separated   Salt to taste
6 tbs. milk   Butter
3 bananas

*Beat whites and yolks of eggs separately, add milk to
yolks, and fold in whites. Slice bananas in rounds and add
with salt to beaten eggs. Melt butter in skillet. Add egg
mixture, covering before turning, so that bananas will
steam. Turn and cook the other side. (When eggs begin to
set, I place a soup plate over the skillet, turn the omelet
quickly into it and flop it over on the uncooked side.
It's easier for me than using a spatula. You could cook the
topside under the broiler or in oven, if you prefer.)
Serves four. This may be made into a sweet omelet by
adding rum and sugar, then setting aflame. A nice trick for
you with chafing dishes.*

ଛ In Mexico this would probably be served with
tomatoes, as a vegetable. An astonishing combination,
you may think, but really quite pleasant.

VEGETABLES

MEXICAN BEANS
ᔋᔋ *Frijoles*

Frijoles are a Mexican tradition, and appear in some
form or other at every meal in Mexico. Yes, even at
breakfast! They are a necessary part of many of the
typical Mexican dishes, such as tostadas. In this
country Mexican pink beans are always used, though
Mexicans use a small red bean. It is not necessary to
soak the beans before cooking.

*Put 2 cups of Mexican pink beans on to cook in 5 cups of
lukewarm water, cover, and cook gently until tender
(about 1½ to 2 hours). Stir beans occasionally, and do not
add salt until the last ½ hour of cooking time. Heat
½ cup of bacon drippings, oil, or lard in a frying pan.
(Bacon drippings add flavor.) Add the beans, a few
spoonfuls at a time, mashing them well into the fat, then
add some of the bean liquid, repeating until the
beans and liquid have been used. Continue cooking and
stirring until the beans are the desired consistency. You will
probably have to add more fat during the frying. If you
have a deep freeze, it is wise to make a big batch of these
and freeze some for future use.*

*Frijoles refritos are simply fried beans fried again in
additional fat, and frijoles chinitos are refried refried beans!*

38

Cubes of Monterey Jack cheese added to the beans and allowed to melt make a delicious variation, as does crumbled, fried chorizo (Mexican sausage). Chopped sautéed onions, green pepper, and garlic is a good addition too, along with a little chile powder dissolved in hot stock. A favorite Mexican addition is pieces of sardines and strips of green chiles. Any of these variations would make a fine hearty entrée of the beans.

ᕃᕍ Frijoles are a natural accompaniment to many of the characteristically Mexican dishes given in this book, but we shall be very disappointed if you don't try serving these savory beans with traditionally American menus, too. They are wonderfully good with barbecued steak or hamburgers as a change from potatoes. And do pass a bowl of thick sour cream to spoon over them.

WHITE BEANS, SPANISH STYLE
ᕃᕍ *Alubias Blancas a la Española*

Unlike the Mexican frijoles, these beans must be soaked overnight, then cooked slowly in fresh water to which salt and pepper are added from the start. Sometimes I add some salt pork when I'm cooking the white beans. It adds good flavor.

1 lb. dry white beans	*2 tbs. oil*
Salt and pepper to taste	*1 lb. fresh tomatoes, peeled*
1 medium-sized onion,	*and chopped*
chopped	*1 tbs. minced parsley*

Fry onions, tomatoes, and parsley together in hot oil, then add the cooked beans with their juice and let simmer to a cream consistency.

DRY RICE SOUP WITH GARBANZOS
⁊❧ Sopa Seca de Arroz con Garbanzos

In the section on Soups I explain how these dry soups
are used in Mexico. Most Americans would choose
to serve them as entrées. This one is a most delightful
way to serve garbanzos, sometimes called chick-peas.
I usually buy the canned ones to save time and bother.

½ cup oil
1 clove of garlic
1 cup uncooked rice
2 tbs. minced onion
½ (8-oz.) can tomato sauce

1 can garbanzos
2 ¼ cups boiling broth or
   water
Salt and pepper to taste

*Brown garlic clove in hot oil, then discard. Fry rice until
just golden, remove excess oil. Add minced onion, tomato
sauce, garbanzos, and season. Pour boiling broth or
water over this, cover tightly, and cook slowly for
30 minutes, without peeking until time is up. For variation,
1 package of frozen peas and 1 can of chopped pimientos
may be added to the above. Serves six.*

STRING BEANS, MEXICAN STYLE
⁊❧ Ejotes a la Mejicana

A good vegetable to serve with fried or broiled chicken.

1 lb. string beans, cut
   lengthwise
3 tbs. oil
2 tbs. minced onion
1 cup tomato puree

1 minced green peeled chile
   (or bell pepper, if you
   must)
1 cup chicken or beef broth
Salt and pepper to taste

*Fry onion and chile in hot oil. Add tomato puree, green
beans, and then broth. Season, cover tightly, and cook
until beans are just tender. A little oregano rubbed between
the palms of the hands is a pleasant addition. Serves four.*

STRING BEANS WITH PIMIENTOS

ह*ั Ejotes con Pimientos Morrones*

Pimientos morrones are nothing more nor less than
the large sweet red peppers you all can buy in cans.
Of course, if you are lucky enough to find them, and
industrious enough to roast and peel them, fresh sweet
red peppers may be used. (See chiles rellenos, p. 63.)

1 lb. string beans	*3 red pimientos, cut in strips*
2 tbs. olive oil	*1 tbs. minced parsley*
2 tbs. minced onion	*Salt and pepper to taste*

*Either French-cut or slice beans and cook until just
barely tender in boiling, salted water. Fry the onion in oil
until transparent, add cooked, drained beans, pimientos,
and parsley. Fry together lightly, season, and if necessary
add a little broth or hot water. Garnish platter with
slices of hard-cooked egg. Serves four.*

ह*ั Red and green, here is a vegetable that lends
color as well as savor, yet is simple and easy to prepare.

PEAS WITH LETTUCE AND HAM

1 tbs. butter	*¼ cup water*
1 small onion, minced	*1 small head of lettuce,*
½ cup chopped raw ham	*chopped*
1 lb. shelled peas	*Salt and pepper to taste*

*Wilt onion in butter, add ham, peas, and water. Cover
and cook until peas are almost tender. Add the lettuce and
complete cooking, shaking the pan, not stirring. Serves six.*

ह*ั Pois à la Française à la Elena!*

SWISS CHARD, SPINACH, STRING BEANS

After cooking, these three vegetables may be served in
a most appetizing manner thus:

*Sauté drained vegetables with chopped green onion in
olive oil. Season to taste.*

ASPARAGUS SPANISH

2 lbs. asparagus
2 tbs. butter
1 small onion, minced
1 small bay leaf
Salt and pepper
3 tbs. flour

2 cups chicken or veal stock
Pinch of nutmeg
2 egg yolks
1 tbs. lemon juice
1 tbs. additional butter

Tie cleaned asparagus into bunches for individual servings, and cook until just barely tender. Melt butter, add onion, bay leaf, salt and pepper, and cook without browning. Then add flour, stock, and nutmeg, and let simmer for 20 minutes. Beat egg yolks until very light and mix with lemon juice. Strain sauce, return to saucepan, and put on very low fire, making certain it does not boil. Gradually add egg yolks and lemon juice and the 1 tablespoon of butter. Serve asparagus on toast with sauce poured over. Serves four generously.

ᢧ A nice change from asparagus Hollandaise for us asparagus lovers, and nothing tricky to worry about.

ZUCCHINI TORTE

Other cooked vegetables such as green beans, spinach, or broccoli may be used in place of zucchini. Sometimes I use Parmesan instead of Cheddar cheese. It's good, too.

2 lbs. small zucchini
¼ cup grated Cheddar
   cheese

1 cup milk
3 egg yolks
Salt and pepper to taste

Boil whole zucchini until just tender, then slice. In deep oven dish put a layer of zucchini covered with a layer of grated cheese, salt and pepper, until all vegetables are used. Beat egg yolks well with milk and pour over zucchini. Bake in 350° oven until eggs and milk are set. Serves six.

ᢧ Kissing cousin of Italian frittata is this beguiling recipe of Elena's.

SPINACH TORTE

2 packages frozen spinach,
   or like amount of fresh
   spinach
1 can mushroom soup
1/4 cup milk

2 eggs, well beaten
2 tbs. grated Parmesan
   cheese
Butter
Salt and pepper to taste

Cook spinach, chop fine, and drain well. Combine the soup with the milk, then add the eggs and cheese. Mix the seasoned spinach with this, pour into a well-greased casserole, dot with butter. Bake at 350° about 1/2 hour, or until set. Serves eight.

VEGETABLE TORTE WITH WHITE SAUCE

This dish will take care of both potato and vegetable dish in one. It may be varied by substituting vegetables other than the peas and carrots suggested here.

1 cup mashed potatoes
1 cup cooked peas
1 cup diced cooked carrots
3 eggs, well beaten
1/2 cup grated cheese

Salt and pepper to taste
Fine bread crumbs
1 or 2 cups medium white
   sauce

Mix potatoes with vegetables, add eggs and cheese. Season, and pour into mold which has been buttered and sprinkled with bread crumbs. Dot top with butter and bake at 375° for 45 minutes, or until firm in center. Turn out from mold and serve hot, covered with white sauce. Let stand a few minutes, then cut like cake to serve to six.

⇛ Versatile indeed is this dish, which could be made hearty enough to spring on your family for Lent with the addition of bits of leftover fish, more cheese, or, or, or?

43

BROCCOLI MAYONNAISE

"Nadie muere de cornada de burro."
"You will never die by the horns of an ass."

Once a Mexican girl who was my dinner guest
confessed that she had never eaten broccoli and was
curious to taste it. I fixed it this way and anxiously
awaited her reaction, which seemed slow in coming.
Finally she said in amazement, "Why, it's sweet!"
Alas, someone had switched currant jelly for the
mayonnaise on my cupboard shelf! The broccoli must
have looked as queer as it tasted.

Cooked broccoli	*Celery salt to taste*
1 clove of garlic	*Mayonnaise*

*Keep cooked broccoli hot. Rub a hot platter with a
cut clove of garlic. Spread mayonnaise on platter. Sprinkle
celery salt and pepper over broccoli and turn out on platter,
rolling in mayonnaise until well coated. Serve quickly.*

ε► Elena is fond of saying:

"A la mejor cocinera se le va un tomate entero."
"The best of cooks will sooner or later pull a boner."

Why not surprise and delight your guests or family
sometime by serving this separately as a first course
in lieu of salad?

CARDOON

Sometimes known as cardoni, this little-used vegetable
may be found in season in most Italian markets. This
is a recipe for the chafing dish, but may be done
just as well (though perhaps not quite so effectively)
in your double boiler. If the preliminary preparation
seems too much trouble, buy your cardoon in cans.

1 cardoon	4 large cloves of garlic
1/2 lb. unsalted butter	(left whole)
1/2 cup olive oil	1/2 lb. Italian anchovies

The cardoon is cut into 1-inch slices and boiled in salted water until tender, after first discarding rough outside leaves and scraping to remove strings. Keep it hot until serving time. Place butter and olive oil in top part of chafing dish or double boiler, put over flame until butter is melted, then add garlic cloves (remove these at serving time). Sauté until very lightly browned, then place over hot-water pan, keeping water boiling below. Now add Italian anchovies and stir until dissolved. These anchovies, also purchased at Italian markets, are prepared by soaking in water for a few minutes, then scraping off scales, and carefully opening down back after removing head, tail, and backbone. Rinse and dry thoroughly before adding to sauce. Place a serving of cardoon on plate and pour sauce over. Do not mix the two in the chafing dish.

৯ Kudos to Elena for this truly gourmet recipe! We hope it will inspire some of you to search out this rough- and tough-looking fellow, the cardoon, distant relative of the artichoke.

SMALL NEW POTATOES

1 1/2 lbs. very small new	1 cup broth
potatoes	1 tbs. dark prepared mustard
4 tbs. butter	(not yellow, please!)
3 egg yolks	Salt and pepper to taste

Boil the potatoes in their jackets, peel, and fry in butter. Mix egg yolks, mustard, and broth, and cook gently until it begins to thicken. Add the potatoes and let simmer for a few minutes. Season, and sprinkle with minced parsley. Serves four.

ᗌᕈ Superb accompaniment to almost any entrée (try it with a cold one!), this recipe fills us with a nostalgia for broiled chicken and the first asparagus of the season. Ah, spring!

POTATO BALLS

Big brothers to the little potato balls used in soups, these are made from one part cream-puff dough to two parts mashed, baked potatoes. These may be made a day before using and fried shortly before dinner.

*3 medium-sized baked
  potatoes
½ cup water
2 tbs. butter*

*½ cup flour
2 eggs
Salt and pepper to taste*

Scoop potatoes from shells while hot, and mash smooth. Measure out 2 cups of potatoes, loosely packed, and to them add this batter: Boil water with butter, add flour all at once, and mix well until it separates from sides of pan. Add unbeaten eggs, one at a time, beat well, and season after mixing with potatoes. Shape into balls resembling small potatoes, roll in flour, and deep-fry in hot oil. If you choose, you may add the 1 tablespoon of chopped parsley and the 2 tablespoons of grated Parmesan called for in the soup version of these. Makes 18 to 20 portions.

ᗌᕈ Esthetic appeal plus appetite appeal is the rightful boast of these feathery-light little potato balls. Let them grace your next roast.

fish

BAKED FISH WITH ALMONDS

2 lbs. cod or haddock
(6 slices)
¼ cup oil
½ cup almonds, blanched
and browned in oven
1 small onion, minced
3 tbs. minced parsley

1 bouillon cube dissolved in
2 tbs. water
2 tbs. lemon juice
1 small onion, sliced
1 bay leaf
Thyme to taste
6 peppercorns

*Chop almonds fine and put in saucepan with oil, minced
onion, parsley, and stock. Simmer slowly for 5 minutes,
remove from heat, and add lemon juice. Place sliced onion,
bay leaf, thyme and peppercorns in greased shallow
baking pan. Place fish over seasonings, pour almond mixture
over top, and bake uncovered in 350° oven for
35 to 45 minutes. Serves six.*

ৡ Fish and almonds have always been good
together, but never better than here.

RED SNAPPER
ৡ *Huachinango*

In Mexico this fish is served often and in many
different ways. On my last visit to Mexico, at a lovely
restaurant in Xochimilco, I enjoyed red snapper slices,

47

floured and fried, served with a sauce made by simmering together chopped green onion, fresh tomatoes, skinned and chopped, oregano, lime juice, and chile tepín (little red-hot chiles).

BLACK BASS, SPANISH STYLE

The tomatillo called for here is a variety of tomato the size of a walnut, light green in color, and delicious in flavor. It is not yet too well known, but is available in all Mexican stores when in season and can now be obtained in cans. Remove the thin skin before using.

6 slices bass	½ cup oil
2 cups tomatillo	¼ cup vinegar or lemon
1 cup parsley, minced	juice
2 large onions, chopped	Salt, pepper, and cloves to
2 mashed cloves of garlic	taste

In a well-buttered casserole place a layer of tomatillo, parsley, and onions; then one of raw fish, a little of the oil, seasonings, and vinegar. Repeat until all ingredients are used, and bake in 350° oven for 30 minutes. Garnish with pickled wax chile peppers and green or ripe olives. Serves six.

ટ્ટે Black bass may not always be obtainable, but we see no reason any similar-textured white fish would not serve here, as even a piece of old cardboard should taste good in this sauce. As an old Mexican proverb says:

"Cuando se revuelve el agua cualquier ajolote es salmón."

"When times are tough a hot dog is as good as a steak";

or, literally,

"When water is riled any ajolote appears to be a salmon."

48

An ajolote is a sort of amphibian (a newt- or salamander-type creature) used as food for many years in Mexico. No, Elena does not include a recipe for ajolote.

HALIBUT WITH CAPERS

2 lbs. halibut in one piece
⅓ cup oil
1 small onion, minced
2 mashed cloves of garlic
1 cup tomato puree, or fresh
   chopped tomatoes
⅓ cup capers
1 tbs. vinegar or lemon juice
1 bay leaf
Chopped green chiles
   (canned or fresh) to taste
Salt and pepper to taste

Season fish and place in baking dish. In a separate pan heat oil and fry onions slightly, then add tomato and garlic, capers, vinegar, bay leaf, and chopped green chile. Pour sauce over fish and bake at 375° for about 40 minutes. Instead of the chopped green chile, red chiles (colorados) may be used, in which case they must first be toasted, skinned, and veins and seeds removed. Mash them into a paste, add a little water and strain into the sauce. Serves four to six.

SHRIMP FRITTERS

   Risoles de Camarón

"*Camarón que se duerme se lo lleva la corriente.*"
"The sleeping shrimp is carried away by the current";
or,

"Don't go to sleep or the parade will pass you by."

½ cup water
2 tbs. butter
½ cup flour
2 eggs
½ cup grated American
   cheese
1 cup cooked shrimp

*Bring water to a boil with butter, then add flour all at once,
stirring vigorously until mixture leaves sides of pan.
Remove from heat and add well-beaten eggs, beating until
smooth and thick. Stir in cheese and shrimp, and drop
by small spoonfuls into hot shallow fat, basting with fat
until well-browned on both sides. Drain and serve with or
without sauce, allowing 2 fritters for each serving. This
amount makes 12 fritters, or 6 servings, if my
arithmetic is correct.*

ह Elena's arithmetic is perfect, but her judgment
of capacity (at least of ours) seems erroneous in this
case. We could eat at least three of these goodies,
and probably four.

WHITEBAIT

Although I prefer whitebait here, this a good and
different way of preparing almost any fried fish.
Simply roll the fish in flour, salt and pepper, and fry
crisp in oil. Serve with salsa fría, p. 82, and tostadas,
which are crisp-fried raspadas.

COLD FISH WITH GUACAMOLE
ह *Pescado con Guacamole*

I think you will like this combination of flavors, and
the dish is as beautiful to look at as it is delicious
to eat.

1 whole fish weighing 3 to 5 lbs. (I often use mackerel)	*3 cups guacamole (p. 12)*
1 bay leaf	*½ cup pearl onions*
1 clove of garlic	*24 stuffed green olives*
Pinch of oregano	*Peeled green chile peppers*
	1 tbs. vinegar (optional)

50

Leave head and tail on fish. Poach in salted water with bay leaf, garlic, vinegar, and oregano. When cooked, place on platter, removing skin and bones, then reshape with hands and chill. At serving time, cover fish generously with guacamole and garnish with pearl onions, olives, and chile peppers. Arrange a small heart of lettuce from the fish's mouth and stick 3 radish rosettes into the lettuce with toothpicks.

&∾ Elena's very own masterpiece and what a conversation piece to grace your buffet!

CODFISH PATTIES

1 lb. salt codfish	*Salt and pepper to taste*
4 eggs, separated	*1 tbs. prepared mustard*
2 tbs. flour	*Stuffed green olives*
½ cup oil for frying	

Soak the codfish overnight. The following day, drain, add fresh water, and cook very slowly. Drain thoroughly and shred. Beat the whites of eggs until stiff, add the yolks and beat a little more. Season with salt and pepper and fold in the flour and the codfish. Drop by tablespoonfuls in shallow frying pan of hot fat or oil, and cook until brown on both sides. Drain on absorbent paper, spread each patty with mustard, and put an olive in the center. Serves six.

&∾ A new twist to codfish cakes. Serve these very hot with big baked potatoes covered with sour cream flavored with chives, and any green salad.

FISH IN FILBERT SAUCE

Several years ago I had fish in Taxco served with this sauce. For this recipe it is best to use one of the moist, soft types of fish, such as sheepshead, red snapper,

striped or rock bass, or pompano. The fish should be
in rather thick slices, too.

8 thick fish steaks	3 tbs. oil
2 cups white wine	1 slice bread
1 bay leaf	20 filberts
1 small onion, sliced	1 tbs. minced parsley
Sprig of thyme	1 clove of garlic
Oregano to taste	Pinch of saffron (optional)
Salt and pepper to taste	

Poach fish slices in wine with bay leaf, onion, thyme, and
a little rubbed oregano. Fry bread in oil, remove, and
grind with the filberts, parsley, garlic, and saffron, then
return to oil and fry lightly. Add wine in which fish
was cooked, let all boil together for about 5 minutes, and
pour over fish. Serves eight.

&⤳ Filberts or hazelnuts, whichever you call them,
don't miss trying them in this excellent sauce.

EGGPLANT AND CLAM CASSEROLE

1 large or 2 small eggplants	2 (7-oz.) cans minced clams
¼ cup butter, melted	Salt and pepper to taste
4 tbs. flour	Buttered crumbs
1 cup cream or rich milk	

Peel eggplant, cut in chunks, and cook in salted water
until tender, then drain and mash. Make a thick white
sauce by melting butter, stirring in flour, and adding cream
or milk slowly. Add clams and their juice to cream sauce
and cook until thick and smooth. Add eggplant, season,
pour in casserole, and top with buttered crumbs.
Bake 45 minutes in a 325° oven. Serves six.

poultry

SQUABS WITH SHERRY

The inspiration for this dish came from a dinner guest
with a great weakness for ginger. Knowing this,
I decided to try ginger in this recipe, and everyone
loved it.

4 squabs
4 thin slices of bacon
2 cloves of garlic (left
   whole, to be removed
   later)
Rosemary, thyme, oregano
   combined to make 1 tsp.
   in all

1 tsp. ginger
Butter and oil for browning
   (half of each)
Salt and pepper to taste
Broth made from simmering
   giblets and necks
4 tbs. Sherry

*Truss birds and lay a half strip of bacon over each breast.
Heat butter and oil in Dutch oven and brown squabs
well. Add herbs, garlic, and sprinkle with flour. Complete
browning, then add the broth seasoned with ginger and
Sherry. Lay birds breast down and simmer
covered until tender.*

‽• Catering to her guests' food foibles is Elena's
long suit, and what an incredible memory she has for
everyone's pet likes and dislikes!

53

DRUNKEN PIGEONS

🦆 *Pichones Borrachos*

This is an early Mexican recipe. The birds are supposed
to become inebriated on the claret in their sauce.
The original recipe contained sugar, and a tiny bit
might be all right if the wine is cold. Let your
taste buds guide you.

8 pigeons	*2 cups California claret*
4 large tomatoes, peeled	*¼ cup raisins*
1 slice dry toast	*1 cup sliced ripe olives*
¼ cup chopped almonds	*2 tbs. chopped citron*
1 clove garlic, crushed	*Salt, pepper and cinnamon*
2 tbs. minced parsley	

*Brown 8 pigeons in ½ cup bacon fat and put them in a
casserole. In the same pan, fry four large tomatoes, a slice of
dry toast, broken into pieces, the almonds, garlic, and
parsley. After about 5 minutes, add wine, raisins, olives, and
citron. Season with salt, pepper, and cinnamon, pour over
the pigeons, and cook in 325° oven until tender.
Serve with rice, wild or domestic.*

🦆 Any small game birds such as doves or quail
would be equally delicious here. If you have no Nimrod
friends, try Rock Cornish Game hens. The wonderful
sauce should improve what can sometimes be a
rather dry bird.

CHICKEN ROASTED, DRUNKARD STYLE

࿊ॐ *Pollos Borrachos*

Although this recipe appears in my other cook book
I could not resist including it again here as it always
makes such a hit with everyone.

2 (3 lb.) roasting chickens, cut up	1-inch stick of cinnamon
4 tbs. oil	1/4 tsp. cloves
3 onions, cut in rings	1 bay leaf
1/3 cup chopped parsley	2 tbs. vinegar
2 tbs. sesame seed	1/2 cup dry Sherry
4 whole black peppercorns	16 green olives
Salt to taste	4 green peeled chiles, cut in strips, or less, as desired

Heat 2 tablespoons of oil in Dutch oven and put in onion
rings, parsley, sesame seed, peppercorns, cinnamon stick,
cloves, and bay leaf. Now add chickens and pour over
top of chickens the remaining oil, vinegar, and Sherry. Add
the whole olives and green peeled chiles to taste.
Salt, cover oven tightly, and simmer for 1 hour, occasionally
turning chickens lightly, serves eight.

ࣸॐ Varied and wondrous are Elena's many ways
with chicken, and this perhaps most wondrous of all.

CHICKEN WITH RICE

࿊ॐ *Arroz con Pollo*

My Spanish-born mother gave me this traditional
recipe, one of the many heirlooms she left me, bless
her heart.

Oil for frying	1/2 cup tomato puree
1 (3-lb.) chicken, cut in pieces	3 cups chicken broth
Salt and pepper	1 cup raw rice
1 medium-sized onion, minced	3/4 cup peas, if desired
	1/2 tsp. paprika
1 mashed clove of garlic	1 tbs. chopped parsley
	1 small can pimientos

Simmer the giblets and neck in water to make broth. Brown the chicken in hot oil without flavoring it, seasoning well with salt and pepper. Remove chicken and cook onion and garlic for a few minutes gently. Add tomato puree and broth. Return chicken to pan and simmer for 20 minutes, then add rice, peas, and paprika. Cook uncovered about 30 minutes longer, or until all liquid is absorbed and rice and chicken are tender. The chopped parsley and sliced pimientos are added just before serving. This is right to serve four.

As Spanish as castanets is this, and a real culinary classic.

ELENA'S BONED STUFFED CHICKEN

This is my very special company chicken. Once you try boning a chicken you won't find it too difficult, and it does make them look so plumped up and pretty. Order small young chickens and ask your butcher to remove necks and wing tips. Cut the skin down the back and remove the bones with a sharp paring knife, scraping the chicken off the skeleton until only the lower leg bone and upper wing are left. I usually stuff the chickens with the recipe I give here, but picadillo (p. 64) makes a delicious and unusual stuffing, as does the rice filling on the following page. The stuffing recipe given here is for 6 chickens. The picadillo recipe will stuff about 3.

1/4 lb. butter
1 medium-sized onion, chopped fine
1 mashed clove of garlic
1/2 lb. raw ham, cut in small dice (don't remove the fat!)
1/2 lb. fresh mushrooms
2 large French rolls, cut in small pieces
Salt and pepper to taste
1/4 cup half and half (cream and milk), or white table wine

Cook onions and garlic in butter until wilted, add ham,
then chopped mushroom stems, saving the caps to garnish
the chickens. Cook until mushrooms are tender, then
add bread cubes. (This makes them quite juicy.) Season to
taste, and mix in the half and half or table wine. Stuff
the chickens, filling up hollows and shaping with hands.
Rub the birds with butter or oil, and roast at 325°
until tender. Serve chickens whole and split them at table
with poultry shears, allowing ½ chicken per person.

ટેરુ At Elena's we once experienced a memorable
double exposure to these beautiful birds. Not only did
we have the joy of beholding and consuming the
finished product, but also the fun of watching Elena
deftly probing with her nimble fingers for each tiny
bone, never tearing the flesh. Spectacular!

CHICKEN STUFFED WITH RICE

"Grano a grano llena la gallina el buche."
"Grain by grain the chicken fills its craw."

This makes a fine alternate stuffing for the boned
chickens above. The amount given here should be right
for 1 large or 2 small chickens.

1 (4- or 5-lb.) roaster
2 cups chicken broth made
* from giblets and neck*
⅓ cup oil
1 cup raw rice
½ cup blanched almonds,
* ground*
¼ cup tomato puree
1 tbs. minced onion
2 tbs. minced parsley
½ tsp. oregano
2 tbs. butter
Salt and pepper to taste

Simmer giblets and neck in water to make broth. Have
chicken broth boiling. Brown rice in oil; then add almonds,
tomato puree, onion, parsley, and boiling broth. Season
to taste, rubbing oregano between palms of hands, cover,

*and cook until rice is tender. Stuff chicken, rub
with butter, and roast in 325° oven.*

ટ૦ Such a pleasant change, this stuffing. Whatever
has happened to baked stuffed chicken that used to
appear as regularly as Sunday? Today too few birds
seem to survive the frying age.

TURKEY WITH CHESTNUTS, SPANISH STYLE

Here is a good recipe for the new small turkeys which
have appeared in the markets fairly recently. Don't
try it with a very large bird.

1 small turkey, cut up	*1½ cups chicken broth*
Juice of 2 lemons	*(or turkey)*
Salt and pepper	*¾ cup dry Sherry*
½ cup oil	*24 chestnuts, shelled and*
1 large onion, minced	*blanched*
¾ cup cubed raw ham	*¾ cup blanched almonds*

*Pour lemon juice over the turkey pieces, sprinkle with
salt and pepper, and brown in oil. Add the onion, ham,
broth, and Sherry, cover and cook slowly. Shell and blanch
chestnuts and put through food chopper with the blanched
almonds. To shell chestnuts easily, cut a slit in each nut,
place in a heavy frying pan with a little oil, and heat
about 10 minutes, shaking pan. Remove shells and skins
with a sharp knife. When turkey is almost done, add
the paste of chestnuts and almonds and continue cooking
until tender. A good-sized chicken may replace
the turkey with equally delicious results.*

ટ૦ A brand new vehicle for that pair who have
been going around together for so long—turkey and
chestnuts. This is rich. It would be best to keep the
rest of your menu simple.

MEXICAN TURKEY BALLS

ё~ Albóndigas de Guajolote

Of course chicken is just as good in this recipe, but
you are more apt to have leftover turkey than chicken,
and this is an excellent way to use it. A smaller
version of these makes a marvelous hot hors d'oeuvre.

3 slices bread	*1 tsp. ground coriander*
3 cups chopped cooked	*¼ tsp. cloves*
turkey	*2 tbs. butter*
1 clove garlic	*2 qts. boiling salted broth*
3 eggs	*¾ cup almonds, blanched*
1 tsp. salt	*and finely ground*

*Soak bread in a little of the hot broth; then drain well.
Grind the turkey, garlic, and bread, add the eggs and
seasoning, mix well, and form into balls the size
of a walnut. (You may find that you need more bread to
make the mixture stick together well.) Add the butter to the
boiling salted stock, drop in the turkey balls, and simmer
about 20 minutes. Remove the balls with a skimmer. Allow
the broth to boil down about one third; then thicken
with the ground almonds. Return the turkey balls to the
broth to heat. At serving time minced green chiles or green
pepper may be added. Serves four or five. An additional
¼ cup of blanched almonds is a good addition to
the turkey balls themselves.*

ё~ Here is a delicately different means of disposing
of the remains of that holiday bird.

PARTY CHICKEN

Now that we can all buy chickens by the piece you
may wish to use your favorite parts of 2 chickens when
serving this to guests rather than the 1 roaster called
for in the recipe.

1 (5-lb.) roaster, cut in
    pieces
Flour, salt, pepper
Oil and butter
½ lb. fresh mushrooms
1 small onion, minced

1 small mashed clove of
    garlic
¼ cup rich broth
½ cup sour cream
½ cup thick sweet cream
Salt and pepper to taste

Simmer chicken giblets and neck in a little water to make
the ¼ cup broth. Shake the chicken pieces, a few at a
time, in a paper bag with flour, salt and pepper. Pour oil
about ¼ inch deep in heavy skillet, heat, and brown
chicken pieces. Butter a roasting pan generously, arrange
chicken in it, dot with butter, and pour the broth over
all. Bake in a 350° oven about 45 minutes, or until tender.
Shortly before serving time melt 2 tablespoons of butter,
add sliced mushrooms, onion, and garlic. Cover pan
and cook about 5 or 10 minutes, then add both sweet and
sour cream, salt and pepper, and heat almost to
boiling. Place chicken on hot platter and pour sauce over it.

૏ Salubrious, simply salubrious! Noodles or rice—
either is nice.

VERY SPECIAL CHICKEN AND NOODLES

The chicken in this recipe may be cooked the day
before, if desired, and the meat removed from the
bones and added to the sauce.

Oil or butter for frying
Flour, salt, pepper
1 (4-lb.) chicken, cut up
2 large onions, minced
⅓ cup minced parsley
¼ cup chopped celery
1 large mashed clove of
    garlic

1½ cups soup stock or
    canned consomme
½ tsp. Worcestershire sauce
¼ tsp. paprika
½ lb. fresh mushrooms, or
    1 large can
1 (12-oz.) package of wide
    noodles
Salt and pepper to taste

60

Shake pieces of chicken in paper bag with flour, salt, and pepper, then brown in hot oil or butter and place in large pan. Combine other ingredients, except mushrooms and noodles, and simmer with chicken for 1 hour. Cook noodles in boiling salted water, and drain. Add mushrooms to sauce. Place chicken pieces on hot platter, surround with noodles, and pour sauce over all. Serves six.

ह With a tomato aspic chilling in the refrigerator and this toothsome dish heating in the oven, you are all set for a relaxed preprandial drink with your guests.

MEXICAN-STYLE CHICKEN STEW
ह *Guisado de Pollo*

Oil for frying	*1 mashed clove of garlic*
1 (5-lb.) roaster, cut in pieces	*1 medium onion, minced*
½ lb. raw ham, cubed	*¼ cup minced parsley*
2 chorizos (Mexican	*¼ lb. fried almonds, ground*
sausage) or about ¼ lb.	*1 pinch cloves*
1 No. 2 can solid pack	*¼ tsp. cinnamon*
tomatoes	*¾ cup white table wine*

Brown the chicken well in oil, add ham and chorizo which has been removed from its casing, and fry for a few minutes. Add tomatoes, garlic, onion, parsley, almonds, cloves, and cinnamon, and simmer. Put in the wine 15 minutes before chicken is done. Garnish with capers and pickled wax peppers. This serves six.

ह As rich and wondrous a chicken concoction as you ever tasted. With a bowl of fluffy white rice and a salad you have a meal to make culinary history.

ELENA'S CHICKEN AND CORN CASSEROLE
ह *Cazuela de Gallina y Elote a la Elena*

Here again you may prefer to remove the cooked chicken from the bones in large chunks before adding to the sauce.

1 (5-lb.) fricassee chicken,
  cut up
2 onions, minced
2 green peppers, minced
1½ tbs. flour
1 No. 2 can solid pack
  tomatoes

1 mashed clove of garlic
24 pitted ripe olives
7 ears of corn cut from cob,
  or 2 cans whole kernel
  corn
Salt and pepper to taste

Remove excess fat from chicken and render. Simmer
chicken in water until tender. Fry onions and green pepper
in chicken fat, stirring in the flour. Add tomatoes,
garlic, ripe olives, and corn, seasoning to taste. In greased
casserole place alternate layers of chicken and tomato
mixture, covering top with the latter. Bake until brown in
350° oven, about 45 minutes. Serves eight.

CHICKEN IN PARSLEY SAUCE

This recipe was a case of necessity's being the mother
of invention. I once had drop-in guests and had to
stretch my entrée. Remembering my lettuce trick with
peas and ham, I decided to try it here.

Oil for frying
1 large roaster, cut up
¼ lb. lean pork cubes
¼ lb. raw ham, cubed
1 small onion, minced
2 tbs. capers

1 medium-sized bunch
  parsley, chopped
1 small head of lettuce,
  cut up
3 cups water
1 tbs. vinegar
Salt and pepper to taste

Fry roaster in hot oil with cubes of ham and pork.
Remove meat, and in same oil fry onion, parsley,
and lettuce, until partially wilted. Add water, vinegar, salt
and pepper, and bring to a boil. Thicken sauce, if you wish.
Add chicken and other meat, cover, and simmer until
tender. Serves six to eight.

ENTRÉES

CHILES RELLENOS

Through my years of cooking for Americans, I have
done considerable adapting of Mexican dishes to make
them more suited to the American taste. This recipe is
a good example, as these are my very own chiles
rellenos, and extremely popular with everyone. They
are much lighter and fluffier than those made in
Mexico, where a thinner batter is used. Either canned
peeled green chiles or fresh ones may be used, but the
fresh chiles must first be roasted until they blister, then
popped hot into a paper bag to steam for about 15
minutes, so that the outside skin may be easily peeled
off. Canned chiles are less trouble, always available,
and taste just as good here, so why not. Each chile
should be cut into two or three strips, and all seeds
should be removed. Quantities here depend entirely on
how many persons you wish to serve, and how large
their appetites.

Monterey Jack cheese, cut   *Canned or fresh green chiles,*
into domino-sized pieces   *each cut into 2 or 3 strips*

*Wrap a piece of chile around each piece of cheese. Roll
in flour.*

*Make a batter like this, allowing 1 egg to each 2 whole
chiles, and 1 tablespoon of flour to each egg:*

*Beat whites of eggs until stiff, then fold in lightly beaten
yolks and then the flour. Drop the stuffed and floured
chiles into the batter one at a time. Pick up each with a
spoon and transfer to a saucer; then slide from saucer into
about 1½ inches of moderately hot oil in your frying
pan. This keeps the chiles neater and holds more of the
batter. Baste with hot oil or they may turn turtle. Fry until
golden brown on each side, but work quickly! Drain
them well on absorbent paper and let stand. Don't worry
if the nice puffy coating deflates. It will puff up again
when heated in this thin sauce before serving.*

*Fry lightly in a little oil a small onion, minced, and a
mashed clove of garlic. Into the mixture force through
a sieve 2 cups of solid pack tomatoes and add 4 cups
of stock. Allow to boil, then season with salt, pepper, and a
teaspoon of oregano, rubbed between the palms of the
hands into the sauce. At serving time put the peppers in the
boiling sauce for about 5 minutes.*

ঌ Don't let these scare you. They are really fun,
though we must admit we marvel at the ease and
neatness with which Elena turns them out. We found
that our little ⅓ cup measure was a real aid here—
even better than Elena's saucer. Put a little batter in
the measuring cup, add the chile, and cover with
batter. Slide all into the hot oil with your very clean
forefinger, and your chiles will all turn out the same
size. The real joy of this dish is that it can be made
days ahead of time, and heated in the sauce at dinner
time. These chiles freeze perfectly.

PICADILLO

Picadillo is a sort of hash, somewhat like mincemeat,
which is used for many Mexican dishes. I call it
"fancy hash" and use it in many ways: as a stuffing,

for an empanada filling, for tacos, or for a delightful poultry dressing. When used to stuff a chicken it is nice to substitute raw, plumped prunes for the raisins. The recipe as given here is right for entrées, but the sugar and spices should be increased when it is to be used for dessert empanadas. Mexicans often use boiled meat for picadillo, or a leftover pot roast, or what have you?

1 lb. ground beef or pork
1 medium-sized onion, finely chopped
3 tbs. oil (omit for pork)
2 large fresh tomatoes, skinned and chopped, or
1 cup solid pack tomatoes
1 mashed clove of garlic
2 tbs. vinegar
1 tsp. sugar

1 tsp. cinnamon (or more)
Pinch of ground cloves
¼ tsp. ground cumin (optional)
1 tsp. salt
½ cup seedless raisins plumped in
¼ cup hot stock
½ cup blanched, slivered almonds

Brown the meat and onion, add remaining ingredients, tossing almonds in last. Simmer about a half hour.

STUFFED PEPPERS WITH PICADILLO
ࣷ Chiles Rellenos con Picadillo

Fresh green chile peppers for this recipe, as the stems must be left on. Place the chiles under the broiler and turn on all sides. When they are well blistered, place in a paper bag and close tightly to let them steam for 15 minutes. Peel off the skin and remove seeds, being careful not to break the chiles. Stuff with the picadillo recipe above, dip in batter, fry in hot oil, just as for the chiles stuffed with cheese.

1 dozen fresh long green chiles (or bell peppers, if you must)
1 recipe for picadillo

Oil to fry
6 eggs, separated
6 tbs. flour
Salt to taste

*Beat whites of eggs until stiff, then fold in lightly beaten
yolks and then the flour. Stuff the chiles with picadillo
and carefully drop into the batter. Fry in about 1½ inches
of hot fat until golden brown, either basting the top
with hot oil or immediately turning the chiles. Otherwise
you may find it difficult to keep them right side up.
Drain on absorbent paper and let stand. Before serving time,
make a thin sauce this way: Mince a small onion and
a clove of garlic and fry in 2 tbs. oil. Add a cup of tomato
puree to this, and 4 cups of stock, preferably chicken. When
the sauce is boiling, season with salt, pepper, and a
teaspoon of rubbed oregano, then put in the peppers just
long enough to heat them through, about 5 minutes.
Peppers puff up when heated this way, so they may be
prepared several hours or even a day ahead of time.*

ප This isn't exactly the dish to whip up
from scratch after a long day's shopping, but like its
first cousin, chiles rellenos with cheese, it has the
saving grace of freezing well. The unusual combination
of the spicy picadillo with the gentle bite of the green
chile is pretty exciting. Incidentally, you may have
discovered that green chiles, either fresh or canned,
can be full of surprises. Three may taste mild as a bell
pepper, while a fourth from the same batch may find
you reaching for your hankie. But like people, they are
more fun that way, we think.

ONIONS STUFFED WITH PICADILLO
ප *Cebollas Rellenas con Picadillo*

Here is picadillo, or "fancy hash" starred again. And
again, these onions may be prepared ahead of time and
reheated in the oven just before serving. Obviously

66

the onion in the picadillo recipe should be omitted here. Just add some chopped onion from the centers you scoop out.

12 large onions, parboiled
    until just barely tender
3 tbs. oil
4 eggs
Salt and pepper to taste
Oil or fat for frying

Picadillo (same amount in
    recipe on p. 64) omitting
    onion and cinnamon and
    adding ½ cup chopped
    parsley and 2 tbs. chopped
    green chile

Scoop centers out of onions and stuff with picadillo. Beat eggs until thick, adding salt and pepper. Dip the onions into the egg, and fry in oil until golden brown on both sides. Serve these onions as is, or with a tomato sauce.

PARADISE RICE TORTE
ⱳ *Torta Paraíso*

Veracruz is the origin of this torte, which makes a delicious main-course dish, or a filling dessert with the variations given here.

1 cup raw rice, cooked in
    milk (rice cooked in
    water, or leftover rice
    may be used)
4 eggs

2 tbs. butter
Salt and pepper to taste
Picadillo (same amount
    given on p. 64)

Beat the egg whites stiff, then add the yolks one by one, beating well after each addition. When well blended, pour in the cooked rice and mix. Butter a spring mold or cake pan well, and cover with a layer of rice first, then a layer of the fancy hash, until all ingredients have been used, ending with a rice layer. Dot with butter and place in a moderate oven until hot and golden.

This torte may be served with a good tomato sauce, or as a dessert when sprinkled with powdered or brown sugar and cinnamon. In the last case, add a few pieces of chopped citron to the picadillo and increase sugar and spices to please your sweet tooth. Serves six or eight.

MEXICAN RICE WITH SOUR CREAM AND GREEN CHILE

&ะ *Arroz con Jocoqui y Chile Verde*

1 cup raw rice	*2 cups sour cream*
1 can green peeled chiles	*2 tbs. butter*
½ lb. Monterey Jack cheese	*Salt and pepper to taste*

Cook the rice in boiling salted water until just tender. Cut each chile lengthwise into 3 strips. Cut half the cheese into small oblongs, wrapping a chile strip around each piece. Butter a casserole and put a layer of well-seasoned rice, then 2 or 3 stuffed chile peppers. Season with salt and pepper, cover with sour cream, then repeat until all ingredients have been used. The top should be of sour cream, the remaining cheese, grated, and the butter in dots. Put in a 350° oven until browned on top, about 30 minutes. This serves six.

&ะ Chile and rice is savory and nice. Add cheese and sour cream, it's really a dream! With this dish we must confess to sharing a weakness Elena is always lamenting: "Americans want to overdo Mexican food!" Frankly, we like *lots* more chiles, and hence more cheese. That way this recipe can serve as pièce de résistance at a buffet for lots and lots of guests, as a change from the very popular chiles rellenos.

CHILE CASSEROLE PIE

This recipe was given to me by a lady from Santa Rosa, wife of a captain on a Norwegian boat. I don't remember the exact origin of the dish, but it doesn't matter, as long as it is good, and it is. Its base is a sort of pancake.

68

PANCAKES

¾ cup water	1 cup flour
2 tbs. butter	1 tsp. salt
½ cup sharp American cheese, grated	¼ tsp. paprika
	2 unbeaten eggs

FILLING

2 tbs. oil	1 (12-oz.) can whole kernel corn
1 large onion, chopped	
1 green chile (or bell pepper) chopped	1 small can chopped ripe olives
1 mashed clove of garlic	1½ cups cooked, cubed ham
3 tbs. flour	Salt to taste
3 (8-oz.) cans tomato sauce	1 tbs. chile powder
1 (4-oz.) can sliced mushrooms	½ cup grated American cheese

Bring the water and butter to a boil, add the flour all at once, and stir vigorously until a smooth ball of dough is formed. Add the cheese and seasonings and blend, then beat in the eggs, one at a time. Cool and divide into 12 balls about the size of a plum. Each ball has approximately 3 tablespoons of dough, so it is easiest to measure one and model the others to it. This is sticky stuff, so better work on a well-floured board. Pat the balls into pancakes about 3 inches across, place each on a lightly floured square of wax paper, and chill. Brown in about ¼ inch of oil in the skillet, and drain on paper. The filling is made as follows: Cook the chopped onion, pepper, and mashed garlic in the oil until wilted. Blend in the flour, then add the tomato sauce, mushrooms, olives, corn (liquid and all), ham, salt, and chile powder. Bring the mixture to a boil, then put in layers in a large casserole, alternating with layers of the pancakes. Cover the top with grated cheese, and bake at 350° for 25 to 30 minutes, or until bubbly hot. This casserole may be prepared ahead of time and stored in the refrigerator until ready to heat. It will serve eight.

69

⁎ Slanted toward the tamale pie lovers (who must be legion, judging from the myriad recipes for that conglomerate dish that swell the magazine food pages), this one achieves distinction by virtue of these wonderfully delicate and tender little pancakes. As a variation try them layered with chopped ham, chile rolled with Jack cheese, and sour cream.

FILLED PANCAKES WITH SPINACH AND SOUR CREAM

⁎ *Minguiches de Jocoqui*

PANCAKES

1½ cups sifted flour	1½ cups milk
1 tsp. salt	3 large eggs

FILLING

1 medium-sized onion, chopped	2 cups spinach, cooked, chopped, drained, and seasoned
1 tbs. butter	

TOPPING

2 cups thick sour cream	½ lb. Monterey Jack cheese, diced
Salt to taste	

Make thin pancakes by mixing together the flour, salt, milk, and eggs. Fry in butter, one at a time, in a 6-inch frying pan, using a little less than ¼ cup of batter for each, tipping and tilting the pan to make the batter run evenly over the bottom. This makes from 12 to 18 pancakes. Make a filling by cooking the onion in butter until wilted, then adding the finely chopped spinach. Place a spoonful of this filling on each pancake, roll, and place seam side down in a buttered baking dish. Pour the seasoned sour cream over the top, sprinkle with the diced cheese, and bake at 350° for 25 to 30 minutes. Serves about six.

⁎ Here is a delicate blending of flavors, pleasantly mild with some of the more highly seasoned Mexican

dishes, or, for an American buffet party meal, serve
these with baked ham, and perhaps a lobster aspic or a
shrimp salad.

PORK AND MUSHROOM STEW
   ટ≫ *Guisado de Puerco con Hongos*

2 lbs. lean pork	*2 cups stock*
1 cup solid pack tomatoes	*½ lb. fresh mushrooms, or*
1 tbs. capers	*1 (8-oz.) can*
1 tbs. minced parsley	*Salt to taste*
5 peppercorns	

*Cut the meat in cubes and fry until brown. Add the
tomatoes, capers, and peppercorns, then the stock and
parsley. Simmer about 30 minutes, until the pork is
thoroughly done, adding the mushrooms for the last 5
minutes of cooking time. Serve to four with steamed rice
and string beans with pimientos (p. 41).*

ટ≫ Treasure this little gem of a recipe. Certainly it
is a welcome variation from our two steady alternates,
pork roast and pork chops. Mexican as can be, yet
nothing here to cause the high-tension boys a moment's
heartburn.

PORK PUEBLA STYLE
   ટ≫ *Rajas Poblanas*

For a delicious and easy meal, serve this with refried
beans and tortillas.

2 lbs. pork, cut in cubes as	*6 green peeled chiles, canned*
for stew	*or fresh (bell peppers may*
2 tsp. salt	*be used)*
3 large tomatoes, peeled	*1 onion, minced*
and chopped	*1 clove of garlic, mashed*

71

Place the meat cubes in a pan with a little water and cover. Cook slowly until meat is tender, water disappears, and pork is brown and beginning to fry in its own fat. Add the onion and garlic, then the tomatoes, and last the green peeled chiles, chopped coarsely, or bell peppers, or half and half, according to how hot you like it. Allow all to simmer until tender and well seasoned.

ଛ୬ Excellent and simple. But make ours *all green* chiles!

PORK WITH ZUCCHINI AND CORN
ଛ୬ *Carne de Puerco con Calabazitas y Elote*

Here is a splendid one-dish meal, except to Mexicans, who want frijoles with everything, at all times, whether they are full or not.

2 lbs. lean pork	2 green peeled chiles, chopped
Water to cover	(more if you like it hot!)
2 cloves of garlic	1 lb. baby zucchini, sliced
Salt and pepper to taste	into rings
2 tbs. oil	3 ears corn cut from cob, or
1 large onion, minced	1 can whole kernel corn
1½ cups tomatillo (see below)	

Cut the meat into large cubes and cook until partly tender in water to cover with 1 clove of garlic, salt and pepper. While it cooks, make a sauce by cooking the onion in oil until soft, adding the tomatillo (skins removed first), 1 clove of garlic mashed, and about ½ cup of the water in which the pork was cooked. Simmer a few minutes, then put in the chopped green chiles. Drain the meat, add to the sauce, and let simmer about 15 minutes. Add the vegetables and cook another 15 minutes. Tomatillo is a variety of green tomato which can be found at Mexican stores when in season, but is now available canned. Be sure to remove the skins from either the fresh or canned, and use both the pulp and the liquid.

కా As Mexican as the Cisco Kid and Pancho is this team of squash and corn, and as complementary. The supporting players in the production are those perfect running mates—tomatillo and green chile. The acid of the green tomato cuts the nip of the chile. Bring on the tortillas!

SPARERIBS

This is so simple I see no reason for even listing the ingredients. Just cut each rib separately, sprinkle with Ac'cent, salt and pepper, and put in a 300° oven. Every now and then drain the fat and toss the ribs around. That's all I do, drain constantly, allow to brown, never raising the temperature. Serve these with salsa fría, p. 82.

కా Sparerib lovers take notice!
"Más cerca están los dientes que los parientes."
"Our teeth are closer to us than our relatives."

GRILLED MEAT BALLS
కా *Albóndigas Horneadas*

Any of these recipes for albóndigas may be made into smaller balls and used in clear soups or as hors d'oeuvre. However, this particular version of meat balls is really Italian and so doesn't rightly deserve the Spanish name of albóndigas at all.

1 lb. ground beef	1 mashed clove of garlic
1 cup spinach, cooked, drained, and finely chopped	1 egg
	1 tsp. Ac'cent
1/4 cup grated Parmesan cheese	Salt and pepper to taste
	1/2 cup bread crumbs

73

Mix all ingredients well and form into balls the size of a lemon. Roll in bread crumbs and put in a well-greased shallow pan under the broiler (set at 375°), turning occasionally until done—from 15 to 20 minutes.

৯ Wonderful grilled outdoors, and a good way to stretch beef, yet still a party dish.

MEAT BALLS, GUANAJUATO STYLE
৯ *Albóndigas a la Guanajuato*

My special trick when making any of the very popular albóndigas is to soak the bread in hot milk. Sometimes I substitute hot broth. This makes the albóndigas very light and fluffy.

2 hard-cooked eggs	Sprig of rosemary
2 slices stale bread	Salt and pepper to taste
3/4 cup milk, scalded	3 cups stock
1/2 lb. ground beef	1 tbs. chile powder (more if
1/2 lb. ground pork	you like)
Pinch of cloves	2 tbs. grated cheese
Pinch of cinnamon	

Chop the whites and yolks of eggs separately. Soak bread in hot milk, drain well, then mash with the ground meats, chopped yolks of egg, and the spices. Form this mixture into small balls about the size of a walnut. Combine the stock and chile powder, and when boiling add the albóndigas and simmer 30 minutes. Mince the egg whites and add to the sauce. Place all in a casserole, sprinkle with cheese, and heat in a 350° oven about 20 minutes. Serve hot to four, garnished with ripe olives.

৯ Here is a splendid buffet supper dish, with, of course, the ubiquitous frijoles, and perhaps an extravagant salad of baby artichokes in mustard sauce (p. 25), because your entrée was so economical, or just because they are so very good.

ELENA'S SPECIAL SPAGHETTI SAUCE

Perhaps you know that a tablespoon of oil added to the boiling water in which spaghetti or any sort of paste is cooked will prevent it from boiling over.

¼ cup olive oil	2½ tsp. salt
½ cup chopped onion	Pepper to taste
1 lb. ground raw beef	¼ tsp. sugar
2 mashed cloves of garlic	1 sprig each of these herbs:
¼ cup minced parsley	Rosemary
¼ cup dried mushrooms, soaked, then chopped	Thyme (tomillo, in Spanish)
1 (8-oz.) can tomato sauce	Sweet basil
2 cups tomato puree (or canned tomatoes put through a sieve)	1 cup red table wine
	1 cup diced Romano cheese
	Grated Parmesan cheese

Simmer the onion in olive oil for 5 minutes, then add the ground beef and garlic, stirring until the meat is browned. Add parsley, mushrooms, tomato sauce and puree, salt, pepper, sugar, and the herbs. Simmer for 1 hour before adding the wine, then simmer another hour. Serve this sauce with any pasta or rice (delicious!), first adding the diced cheese to the pasta, then dressing with this sauce, and sprinkling all with the grated Parmesan.

ê➤ As certain proof of the popularity of Elena's cooking (as well as the popularity of spaghetti) she had 6,000 requests for this recipe from one advertisement sponsored by a wine merchant.

ELENA'S QUICK SPAGHETTI
ê➤ *Spaghetti Blanco*

My reputation as a cook has been saved many times by this recipe when unexpected company dropped in. With a green salad and a fruit dessert you will have a perfect meal.

| 1 lb. spaghetti, cooked | 2 egg yolks |
| ¼ lb. butter | Grated Parmesan cheese |

Put butter on a hot platter. When it is almost melted, add the well-beaten egg yolks and mix the spaghetti in quickly and thoroughly. Sprinkle generously with grated cheese. For a wonderful variation, use finely chopped walnuts instead of the cheese.

&ep; "*Más vale llegar a tiempo que ser invitado.*"
     "It is better to drop in at the right time
        than to be invited."

As if Elena's reputation as a cook were ever even vaguely threatened!

SAUSAGE SAUCE FOR SPAGHETTI

For the best flavor in sauces and gravies, I have found that garlic should never be browned. I add it after the onion has been wilted in the fat.

½ lb. link sausages, cut in	½ cup water
thirds	2 tbs. sweet basil (see p. 84
1 small onion, chopped	for preparation)
1 mashed clove of garlic	1 chile tepín, mashed
2 (8-oz.) cans of tomato sauce	Salt and pepper to taste

Fry the sausages until brown, drain surplus fat, add onion, and cook until wilted, then add garlic, tomato sauce, water, sweet basil, and chile tepín. Simmer for 1½ hours. Chiles tepines are tiny red dried peppers, very hot, which can be found at practically any grocer's. They are sometimes called chiles pequines. This sauce will be sufficient for a 12-ounce package of any sort of paste: spaghetti, macaroni, noodles.

&ep; This should be in the repertoire of every conscience-stricken cook who has ever blown the food budget to bits. And what exquisite economy!

ITALIAN RICE BALLS
&~ *Arancini*

Arancini is the diminutive of the Italian word
"aranci", meaning orange. No doubt this dish is so
called because of the size and shape of the rice balls.

RICE BALLS

1 cup raw rice
¼ cup melted butter
2 eggs

½ cup grated Parmesan
   cheese
Salt to taste

FILLING

½ cup cubed Swiss cheese
¾ cup cooked, cubed meat
   (leftover roast or boiled
   beef)

2 hard-cooked eggs, chopped
Any favored spaghetti sauce
   to moisten

COATING

2 cups bread crumbs

2 eggs, beaten

Cook the rice until well done, but do not wash it after
cooking. This is important. When the rice is cold, add
melted butter, 2 eggs, and the grated cheese. Mix
thoroughly and allow to stand for several hours or
overnight. Blend the filling ingredients together, then take
some of the rice mixture, form a little cup-like patty in the
palm of your hand, place a tablespoon of the filling in
the center, cover well with rice, and shape into a ball. Roll
the rice balls in bread crumbs, then in the beaten eggs,
again in bread crumbs until well coated, and fry in deep
fat. Serve these hot with extra sauce, or pour sauce
over the balls.

CANNELLONI

The noodle dough, filling, and sauce may each be
prepared in advance and stored in the refrigerator until
ready to use. Some may prefer a white sauce to the
tomato sauce given here. Either is good, but if white
sauce is preferred, ½ pound of cubed Jack cheese

should be sprinkled over the top and the dish baked in a moderate oven until the cheese melts.

NOODLE DOUGH
2 cups sifted flour
1 tsp. salt

2 slightly beaten eggs

CHICKEN FILLING
¼ cup butter
½ cup chopped celery
2 tbs. chopped onion
½ cup chopped parsley

3 cups cubed chicken or
   turkey
½ cup chicken broth
Salt and pepper
½ cup grated cheese

TOMATO SAUCE
1 tbs. oil
1 medium-sized onion,
   chopped
1 mashed clove of garlic
¼ cup chopped green pepper

3 (8-oz.) cans tomato sauce
¼ tsp. oregano
Pinch of thyme
1 or 2 chiles tepines
1 cup chicken broth

Make noodle paste by sifting flour and salt into a bowl, making a hole in the center of the flour and adding the slightly beaten eggs, then stirring with a fork until a stiff dough is formed. Press into a ball and divide the dough into 3 pieces. Roll each into an approximate square foot, then cut each square into quarters, making 12 small squares in all. Drop a few squares at a time into boiling salted water and cook 12 to 15 minutes, or until just tender. Drain, and put them on a cloth. Cook the celery and onion in butter until transparent, add the chicken, parsley, broth, and seasonings and simmer, uncovered, for 10 minutes; then put about ¼ cup of this filling on each square and roll to form a tube. Arrange the cannelloni, seam side down, in a large baking pan, and cover with a tomato sauce, made by simmering the above ingredients. Sprinkle grated cheese lavishly over the top and place in oven to keep warm. Allow two or three for each person served.

ᑫᕙ Here is Elena's version of an old Italian favorite, and very good it is indeed.

CHICK PEAS WITH SAUSAGES
₰ *Garbanzos con Salchichas*

I use canned garbanzos because they are so easy, and
the few pennies saved by buying the dried ones are
used up by the fuel in cooking them. Italian sausages,
called salciccia, are best here, but Spanish or even
American sausages could be used.

4 Italian sausages　　　　　*1 can garbanzos*
1 small onion, chopped　　　*1 tbs. minced parsley*
1 (8-oz.) can tomato sauce

*Fry the sausages until brown. Add onion and cook until
wilted. Then pour in tomato sauce and when it boils add
garbanzos and parsley. Let simmer 25 to 30 minutes.*

₰ A fine family meal with a green salad. Also
grand enough for company with a glass or two of
good red wine.

PAELLA

My Spanish mother gave me the recipe for this old
and justly famous dish. Somehow it always tastes ten
times better when cooked and served in an earthenware
casserole. Another similar very old Spanish favorite is
called arroz con almejas (rice with clams), and is this
same dish, omitting the chicken or squabs and the shrimps.

*⅓ cup oil (olive oil is most
　authentic here)*
*1 fryer or 2 squabs, cut
　in pieces*
1 onion, minced
1 mashed clove of garlic
1 tbs. chopped parsley
*½ (8-oz.) can Spanish-style
　tomato sauce*
2 lbs. clams, steamed

*1 lb. cooked and cleaned
　shrimps*
*3 cups boiling broth (chicken
　stock plus clam broth from
　steaming clams)*
Salt and pepper
*Pinch of saffron, if desired
　(dissolve in a bit of broth
　first)*
1 cup raw rice

79

Brown chicken or squabs in oil, then add onion, garlic, parsley, and tomato sauce. Mix well, put in the steamed clams (shells and all), the shrimps, the boiling broth, and seasonings. Sprinkle in rice. Cook uncovered over a slow fire for 20 or 30 minutes. Do not stir. Before using the clams, steam them in a small amount of water with a pinch of salt and a clove of garlic until the shells open. If fresh clams are not available, substitute two of the 10-oz. cans of whole clams. Canned clams in shells are sometimes available.

ê≈ Pimientos are perfect with this—so Spanish, you know, and so good. Use them either as a garnish, or better, serve a beautiful rosy platter of Elena's pimientos colorados (p. 24).

ALMOND SAUCE FOR TRIPE, CHICKEN, OR FISH

This sauce is wonderful served over almost any meat, fish, or fowl. Try it with albóndigas, or cooked tongue. When serving it with tripe, I cut the tripe into long strips like macaroni before cooking, then add the drained, cooked tripe to the sauce. Delightful!

¼ cup oil
3 slices French bread (not fresh)
1 medium-sized onion, sliced
¼ cup blanched almonds
½ cup unblanched almonds
Sprig of parsley

1 clove of garlic
2 cups chicken broth (and I mean chicken!)
Salt and pepper to taste
¼ cup blanched and slivered almonds

Heat oil. Fry bread until brown, then remove. Sauté onion, blanched and unblanched almonds, and parsley until nicely browned. Cool mixture. Add garlic and fried bread. Put all through food chopper until mixture is very smooth.

*Add chicken broth and seasonings and simmer until
smooth and thick. Just before serving, add the ¼ cup
blanched and slivered almonds.*

ॐ A versatile and sublime sauce which will
transform practically any leftovers into something for
the queen's taste.

GROUND BEEF PATTIES, ELENA STYLE
ॐ *Chuletas a la Elena*

Here is a happy way to make a pound of ground beef
feed eight hungry people—and handsomely, too!
Season your favorite tomato sauce with a little oregano
to serve over these patties, and you have a good,
inexpensive main dish. Or better still, try
them with salsa fría.

1 lb. lean ground beef	*1 ½ cups fine, dry bread*
1 cup finely chopped parsley	*crumbs*
1 cup finely chopped onion	*¼ tsp. Ac'cent*
3 tbs. grated Parmesan cheese	*Salt and pepper to taste*
1 egg	*Salad oil for frying*

*Mix the beef, parsley, onion, cheese, egg, and seasoning.
Shape the mixture into balls. This should make about 16.
Place crumbs on a large sheet of paper. One by one, roll
the balls in the crumbs, then flatten out with the palm of
your hand. Keep patting them and turning them over and
over in the crumbs, until you have a well-crumbed patty
about 3 or 4 inches in diameter. Chill the patties for
½ hour or longer. Heat salad oil in a skillet (about ¼ inch
deep) and fry the patties to a lovely brown on both sides,
adding more oil to the skillet if necessary. Drain on
absorbent paper. These may be fried ½ hour or so before
serving and kept warm in the oven.*

COLD SAUCE
ह‍‍़ *Salsa Fría*

I include this sauce under Entrées, as it is delicious
with any kind of meat, and my favorite for
tostadas, chalupas, crisp-fried tacos, refried beans, etc.

1 No. 2 can solid pack tomatoes	*1 tsp. oregano, fresh if*
1 onion, finely chopped	*available*
1 can peeled green chiles,	*2 tbs. wine vinegar*
chopped	*1 tbs. oil*
1 tsp. coriander (optional)	*Salt and pepper to taste*

Cut up tomatoes very fine; add other ingredients, stir well.

ह‍‍़ "This is wonderful," says Elena, as she says
about every recipe in this book, and of course she
is right, but we think this one particularly wonderful.
The cold piquant sauce over a hot dish is indescribably
delightful. Even catsup addicts will desert their
favorite condiment once they try this over the lowly
hamburger. Perfect for the barbecue enthusiast. Try it
over fish. For our palate, the addition of a can of
tomatillo (whole green Mexican tomatoes) is well
worth a trip to your nearest Mexican grocery store.
These little tomatoes are not ordinary green tomatoes,
and have a peculiar acerbity which we find hauntingly
delicious. Just be sure to remove the "little overcoat,"
as Elena calls it, before adding the tomatillo.

A clove of garlic mashed with the salt is not amiss
here, either.

BEEF TONGUE À LA VINAIGRETTE
ह‍‍़ *Lengua de Res a la Vinagreta*

1 fresh beef tongue	*Parsley*
1 carrot	*1 bay leaf*
1 onion	*Salt and pepper to taste*
2 stalks celery	

*Cook the tongue in boiling water to which the above
ingredients have been added. This may take anywhere from
2 to 3½ hours. Allow the tongue to cool in the broth
before removing skin and root ends. Save that good
broth for a vegetable soup.*

SAUCE FOR TONGUE

1 cup oil
½ cup wine vinegar
1 tbs. chopped parsley
2 tbs. chopped chives
2 tbs. chopped onion

1 tbs. chopped green pepper
1 tsp. paprika
1 tsp. prepared mustard
3 hard-cooked eggs, chopped

*When the tongue is cold, slice it thin. Combine the sauce
ingredients, then arrange overlapping layers of tongue
slices on a serving platter, pour the sauce over them, and let
stand in the refrigerator overnight. Garnish the platter
with pickled pearl onion, green olives, and little
chiles curtidos.*

ቇ Some hot evening serve this forth to your
favorite guests, teamed with vegetable torte,
and preceded by Elena's marvelous sour cream soup.
Sopaipillas (fried bread puffs) too.

RABBIT IN RED WINE

"Vale más que sobre pan y no que falte vino."
"It's better to have bread left over than to run short of
wine."

1 medium-sized rabbit
½ cup oil
½ cup red wine vinegar
1 onion, minced
2 mashed cloves of garlic
¼ lb. salt pork
3 carrots, chopped

*3 medium-sized tomatoes,
  chopped*
*2 bunches green onions,
  chopped*
2 cups red table wine
Salt and pepper to taste

*Cut the rabbit up as for fricassee. Pour over it the oil,
vinegar, onion, garlic, salt and pepper, and allow to
marinate for 24 hours. The following day cut the salt pork
in cubes, and cook until all the fat has been rendered. Add
the chopped tomatoes, onions, and carrots, and simmer for 5
minutes, then add the rabbit and its marinade. Pour red
table wine over all, cover tightly, and cook slowly until
tender. If chicken is preferred, 2 medium-sized
fryers may be substituted.*

୧୭ To anyone who finds hassenpfeffer a bit too
pungent for his palate, this should be a welcome
discovery. Much more delicate, it still retains
the exciting flavor of the former. Elena treats her little
rabbit with loving care, as befits his tender age.

VEAL ROAST WITH FRESH SWEET BASIL

During the summer months, when basil is plentiful,
I wash it and roll it in a cloth to dry, remove the leaves
from stems, chop them with several cloves of
garlic; then place them in a pint jar, and cover with
olive oil. The basil will keep indefinitely this way,
if you make sure that it is always covered with oil.
Delightful with chicken or any meat gravy, a teaspoon
of sweet basil added to French dressing gives
a wonderful variation to your green tossed salad.

5-lb. roast of veal	*3 tbs. sweet basil,*
2 tbs. oil	*chopped*
¼ cup flour, browned	*Salt and pepper to taste*
1 cup rich stock	

*Salt and pepper the roast, adding the oil, and place in
roasting pan in a 325° oven. When the meat starts to
brown, sprinkle it with the browned flour and sweet basil
and roast another ½ hour, then gradually add the cup of
stock, basting occasionally until all liquid is used. Allow 30*

minutes' cooking time to the pound. Sliced fresh
mushrooms, or a can of button mushrooms, may be added
to the gravy. To brown flour, place on a pie tin in a
350° oven and every so often stir with a fork until the
flour is uniformly brown. This is a trick I learned from
my mother. It gives an excellent flavor to gravies.

&~ Elena's cream puff potatoes (p. 46) are just
about perfect with this.

PARTY ROAST
&~ *Asado Festivo*

This is the translation of a recipe given to me by
a lady from Mexico who cooked it for a party of us at
her house. When I was told she was going to boil
the roast, I held my head in horror to think of that
beautiful piece of meat wasted, but when I tasted the
result later, all I could say was, "Wonderful!"

5 to 6 lbs. lean beef, veal, or pork roast	3 mashed cloves of garlic
½ cup oil	½ cup minced parsley
2 No. 2 cans of solid pack tomatoes, or 4 lbs. of fresh	½ tsp. cloves
½ cup chopped onion	½ tsp. cinnamon
	Salt and pepper to taste

*Brown the roast in the oil, then put meat in a large
pan of boiling water, being careful that the water covers
the meat entirely. In the same oil in which the meat was
browned, cook tomatoes and all the other ingredients
together. When the meat is tender and the water reduced
to about 1½ cups, add the tomato mixture, allowing all
to simmer for ½ hour or until well seasoned. Remove meat
from pan and allow to cool. When cold, slice thin and
place in neat layers on an ovenware platter. Pour sauce
over the meat and place in a 325° oven, first covering the
dish with heavy wrapping paper to prevent its becoming
dry. It may remain in the oven for ½ hour, but do not*

*allow it to dry. Serve garnished with strips of pimientos and
green stuffed olives. For extra flavor, lard beef or veal
with ham or salt pork before cooking.*

꒰ Elena's little new potatoes in mustard sauce
seem to us to be tailor-made for this magnificent roast.

TORTOLETAS MEXICANAS

This and the following recipes given in this section
are typically Mexican dishes made from masa, which
is very finely ground nixtamal, the base of tamales and
tortillas. Masa can be purchased by the pound at
Mexican stores. Be sure to use lard in mixing masa,
as other shortening changes the flavor.

"Manteca hace cocina, no Catarina."
"It's lard that makes the dinner, not Katherine."

TORTOLETA

½ cup masa   *2 tbs. sour cream*
2 cups sifted flour   *1 tsp. salt*
2 tbs. lard   *2 eggs*

CHORIZO FILLING

1 medium-sized onion,   *1 green chile pepper, chopped*
   chopped   *(or to taste)*
3 chorizos, skinned (about   *3 cups cooked mashed beans*
   ½ lb.)   *(frijoles)*
¼ cup sour cream   *Salt to taste*

*Make a soft dough by mixing together the masa, flour,
lard, sour cream, and salt. Add the unbeaten eggs, mix
well; then divide the dough into eighths and roll each into
a ball. Flatten the balls into pancakes about 4 inches across
and ½ inch thick; then form into little cups by pressing
the edges up into a rim. Fry these in deep fat until golden
brown, drain, and fill with chorizo filling, made by
simmering the filling ingredients together until the onion*

is soft and the chorizo cooked. *Decorate with sliced radishes, avocados, and Monterey Jack cheese.*

ξ❧ Actually this recipe *makes* easier than it *reads.* A little practice and you will be doing it as easily as Elena, but not as skillfully—no one can!

ENCHILADAS SONORA STYLE
ξ❧ *Enchiladas Sonorenses*

Tortillas, the national bread of Mexico, are the base of enchiladas. These can be found at any Mexican store, or canned ones are available now at most grocers. Hand-made tortillas are becoming rare, but for enchiladas and tacos the machine-made are preferable, as they are tougher and hold their shape better. Chorizos (Mexican sausages) can also be found at Mexican stores, as can several good brands of red sauce for enchiladas. I give a very simple recipe here for red sauce, and one for chorizo on p. 92. Be sure to use a good, *fresh* brand of chile powder, as it does not improve with age. Too many cooks have a tendency to let it remain on the shelf too long.

RED SAUCE FOR ENCHILADAS

3 tbs. oil
2 tbs. flour
1 mashed clove of garlic
2 cups tomato puree
1 cup hot beef stock

2 tbs. chile powder (more if you like)
Pinch of comino (cumin seed) if desired
Salt to taste

Brown flour in oil. Add garlic and tomato puree. Dissolve chile powder in hot stock and stir into tomato sauce. Season, cover, and simmer about 15 minutes. Dip each tortilla into this hot sauce, then fry lightly in hot oil or lard. (I know you won't love me for this, as it makes a terrible mess, but at the end you will be so happy with the result that all will be forgiven.) Remove 6 chorizos from

87

their casings, crumble, and fry without added fat, but do not brown. Cover each fried tortilla with some chorizo and a piece of Monterey Jack cheese. These enchiladas should be stacked, not folded. When all tortillas have been dipped, fried, and covered with chorizo and cheese, pour the remaining sauce over all. The comino will give a delightful Mexican flavor to the sauce, but I have a lot of respect for comino when I use it! Mexicans do not thicken their sauce, and little is served with enchiladas, but Americans want more, and more, and more sauce, so perhaps you will want to increase the recipe. It should be right for a dozen tortillas. This is a good recipe for flour tortillas, p. 97, if you prefer them.

కు We are in favor of plenty of cold beer with these, followed later by a chlorophyll tablet. Most chorizo is somewhat more than just "kissed by the bud of garlic"—the two are having a downright affair! This does not deter us one whit, but should you wish to vary your enchilada filling, picadillo (p. 64) instead of chorizo is often used, or you may prefer the usual cheese and chopped onion, or leftover meat.

Throughout New Mexico and in parts of Texas, stacked enchiladas are almost invariably served with a fried egg perched ceremoniously on top. A needless glorification, we always felt, and one which we did not encounter in Mexico. However, we did enjoy an enchanting tostada dish descriptively called "horseback riders with chaps," which boasted not one but two fried eggs straddling its crisp rim.

GREEN ENCHILADAS
కు *Enchiladas Verdes*

Canned tomatillo, green tomato, available at Mexican stores, is the base of these enchiladas. Mexicans puree the tomatillo, but I like the sauce better

88

unstrained. If you prefer the puree, dip the tortillas in the sauce before frying, as for red enchiladas. I cannot specify how much peeled green chiles should be used, as this depends entirely upon you and the chiles. You may use as much as a whole can or you may run across one hot green chile that is enough for the whole deal. Green Jalapeña sauce may be used in place of the green chiles. It is sold also in tins or jars at many grocers, but is somewhat hotter than most green chiles, so better taste as you go.

1 dozen tortillas
Oil for frying
2 lbs. lean pork, cut in
½-in. pieces

1 mashed clove of garlic
1 small onion, chopped
1 tomato, chopped
Salt and pepper

SAUCE

2 cans tomatillo
3 tbs. oil
1 mashed clove of garlic

Green chiles, finely chopped,
to taste, or Jalapeña sauce
Salt to taste

Fry the tortillas lightly, as these are to be rolled, and must be pliable. Add meat stuffing, roll, and place in a baking dish. Pour the green tomato sauce over all, covering well. To make the meat filling, add 1 clove of garlic and about 6 tablespoons of water to the meat, cover, and simmer until almost tender. Drain off the liquid, and allow the meat to fry with the chopped onion. Let it get crusty. That's what makes it good. Add the tomato and seasonings, and cook a few minutes longer. For the sauce, skin and remove stems from the tomatillo, and pour, liquid and all, into 3 tablespoons of hot oil. Add the mashed garlic, season with salt and either Jalapeña sauce or finely chopped green chiles. Simmer ½ hour to thicken. These enchiladas may be made ahead of time, heated in the oven, and the hot sauce poured over them at serving time. For Fridays Mexicans often roll the enchiladas without meat, cover with cheese, and melt in the oven, or they may be stuffed with hard-cooked eggs and/or chopped ripe olives.

ટ્ફ For our money, if you haven't eaten these
enchiladas, you haven't eaten! Contrary to a rather
common belief, enchiladas are not the every-day staple
of the working man in Mexico but real fiesta food
there, as here. In defense of chiles (as if they needed
any!) we are told that they are simply teeming
with vitamins, chiefly C. Doubtless this is the reason
the poor in Mexico thrive as well as they do
on their diet of frijoles, tortillas, cheese, and chiles.

SWISS ENCHILADAS
ટ્ફ *Enchiladas Suizas*

Mexicans associate the use of cream with a dairy
country—hence the name of Swiss for these enchiladas.
Both these and the rolled green enchiladas may be
frozen successfully by wrapping tightly in corn husks.

1 dozen tortillas
Oil for frying
6 chicken bouillon cubes

3 cups sweet cream, warmed
½ lb. Monterey Jack cheese,
cubed

CHICKEN FILLING
2 tbs. oil
1 medium onion, chopped
1 mashed clove of garlic
2 chopped green chiles
(or to taste)

2 cups tomato puree
2 cups chopped cooked
chicken
Salt to taste

*Fry the tortillas in about 1 inch of hot oil, being careful
not to let them get crisp, as they must be rolled. Dissolve
bouillon cubes in hot cream and dip each tortilla in the
mixture. Cover generously with the chicken filling, roll up,
place seam side down in a baking pan, pour remaining
cream mixture over all. Top with the cheese, add remaining
cream, dip, and bake in a moderate oven for about 30
minutes. The chicken filling is made this way: Fry the
onion in the hot oil until soft, add all other ingredients, and*

90

*simmer about 10 minutes. Slices of avocado, or hard-cooked
eggs, radishes, green or ripe olives—all are attractive
garnishes for enchiladas.*

ह‍ These mild-mannered and delectable enchiladas
should serve to refute a theory too commonly
subscribed to, that all Mexican food is somewhat hotter
than you know what. As a matter of record, while
visiting in Mexico some years ago, we learned
from restaurant menus that if we wanted our
enchiladas extra hot, we should ask for "Texas style."

TORTILLA HASH
ह‍ *Chilaquiles*

Although another recipe for this dish appears in my
other book (*Elena's Famous Mexican and Spanish
Recipes*), I include this one here because it
appeals greatly to American people, is inexpensive, easy
to make, and can be prepared ahead of time. This is
an ideal dish for buffet suppers, and an excellent
way to use stale tortillas. In case you cannot buy
chorizos (Mexican sausages) I give you a simple recipe.

1 dozen tortillas	*Salt to taste*
¾ lb. chorizos	*½ lb. mild cheese*
1 cup finely chopped onion	*1 cup grated Italian cheese*
2 tbs. chile powder (more,	*(Parmesan or Romano)*
if you like)	*1 can pitted ripe olives*
2 cups tomato puree	

*Cut tortillas in eighths (scissors make this easy) and fry
in hot lard or oil. Remove the oil from pan and fry the
chorizos which have been removed from their casings and
crumbled. Make a sauce by frying the onions in a little oil,
then adding the tomato puree, chile powder (fresh!),
and salt. After the sauce is thoroughly heated, place in a
casserole alternate layers of tortillas, cheese, olives, and*

*chorizos, repeating until all the ingredients are used. Pour
the sauce over all. Sprinkle the top generously with the
grated Italian cheese, and put in a moderate oven for
20 to 30 minutes. This amount should serve ten.*

CHORIZO

1 lb. lean pork, coarsely chopped	*1 large clove of garlic, mashed*
2 tsp. salt	*2 tbs. vinegar*
2 tbs. chile powder	*1 tsp. oregano*
	Speck of comino, if desired

*Mix all ingredients. Let stand for several hours. Fry for
about 30 minutes. If you like it hotter, just add more
chile powder.*

&❧ This makes a delightful buffet dish.

TOSTADAS

Tostada is the name given to any fried raspada, which
is a hand-made tortilla with the face peeled off,
available at Mexican stores where tortillas are made.
These little crisp pieces are often served with appetizers
and soups. However, the famous dish I describe here
is also known as a tostada and is the Mexican favorite
of the West Coast. Fry raspadas until crisp and
brown in 2 inches of fat in the skillet, holding them
down with a pancake turner to keep them flat. You now
have tostadas, ready to be covered with spoonfuls
of any of the following combinations, topped
with shredded lettuce, and served warm with cold
sauce (p. 82). As a time-saving hint, the raspadas are
just as good when fried the day before serving
and crisped in the oven just before using.

*I. Mashed fried beans (p. 38) sprinkled generously with
grated cheese; chorizo (Mexican sausage), which has been
removed from its casing, crumbled and fried; and rings of*

zucchini and/or string beans in small pieces, both of which have been cooked until just barely tender, then marinated in vinegar, water, and salt. Shredded lettuce and sauce for all of these.

II. Pickled pigs' feet with beans and cheese. These are a favorite in some parts of Mexico, Jalisco especially.

III. Guacamole with beans and cheese. Chorizo too, if you wish, or ground meat flavored with onion and chile powder. Quantities depend, of course, on how many are to be served, but it may be helpful to know that chorizo from Mexican stores usually comes in 2-ounce balls, enough for two tostadas.

 A symphony in texture and flavor contrast, the tostada is both entrée and salad. Perfect for a festive luncheon or supper (or any other time), little else is needed. This might be the time to indulge in that rich soup or high-caloric divine dessert you have always wanted to try. You will have fun thinking up your own tostada combinations, but do keep it Mexican in flavor, and remember that its charm is contrast, so wed the bland with the spicy, the soft with the crisp.

TAMALES

As tamales are a universal Mexican food favorite, I have devoted an entire chapter to their making in each of my other cook books, but have had so many requests that I have added these two interesting tamale recipes to this book, as well as some general information on tamale preparation.

> *"Al que ha nacido para tamal, del cielo le caen las hojas."*
> "Heaven provides the corn husks for him who was born to be a tamale."

93

TURKEY TAMALES

ૐ *Tamales de Guajolote*

Tamales may sound like a lot of work to make, but
I assure you they're worth it. These, made with turkey,
are especially popular. If you don't want to go to
the trouble of making your own chili sauce, use the
Mexican salsa that comes in cans.

HUSKS

   *Pick over ½ pound of top quality dried corn husks,
discarding any silk and unattractive-looking ones. Cover with
warm water and soak overnight. Drain and keep
moist until used.*

FILLING

2 lbs. cooked turkey meat	1 ½ cups lard
7 cups Quaker Masa Harina	2 tsp. lard
4 cups turkey stock (or water	
plus 3 tbs. of	
chicken concentrate)	

   *Cut turkey in pieces as for salad, and reserve. Combine
Masa Harina, warm stock, and salt. Beat lard until fluffy, add
the masa, and beat, beat, beat. When a little of the mixture,
dropped in water, will float, you've beaten it enough.
Cover bowl with a damp cloth and keep cool until used.*

CHILI SAUCE

¼ lb. dried chiles pasillas	2 tbs. lard
¼ lb. dried chiles Californias	¼ cup Quaker Masa Harina
(chiles anchos)	2 cups turkey stock
1 large clove garlic	2 tsp. vinegar
1 large onion	1 tsp. salt

   *Toast the dried chiles on a griddle, or put them in a 400°
oven for a minute or two. Don't let them burn! They are
ready when they give off a tantalizing nutty odor. Let them
cool, then discard stems, seeds, and light pithy part of
the insides. Now wash them, then cover with 2 cups of water*

94

*and soak for 2 hours. Put in your electric blender and let
them whirl until smooth. Add enough water to make 2 cups,
and reserve. Now puree or mash the garlic and mince the
onion, and cook in the lard until wilted. Add the Masa Harina
and remaining ingredients and cook until thick. Combine
with the chile puree, taste, and add more salt if necessary.
Add the cut-up turkey and set aside until needed.*

TO MAKE TAMALES

*Did you think we'd never come to this? But you must admit
the other procedures weren't too difficult, were they?
Neither is this.*

*Select a wide pliable husk. (If none of them are wide,
simply put 2 or 3 together, but in opposite directions,
overlapping the sides a little and pasting them together with
some of the prepared masa.) Lay the husk on the table,
point at top, and spread with about 2 tablespoons of
the prepared masa, spreading a space about 5 x 5 inches in the
middle of the husk. The masa should come almost to the
edges of the husk. Now put a very heaping tablespoon of the
filling in the middle of the masa, add a small pitted ripe
olive and 2 or 3 raisins, and roll the sides of the husk over the
filling. Over the seam put a narrow piece of husk which has
been spread thinly with masa. Roll the tamale firmly on
a flat surface, holding the ends so that the filling stays in the
middle. Twist ends and tie with a strip of husk, using it as if
it were a string. With scissors clip ends evenly. Arrange on a
rack in a steamer, and cook over boiling water for 1 hour.
Eat at once or freeze. Reheat frozen tamales by steaming for
about half an hour. Makes about 18 tamales.*

FRESH CORN TAMALES

&~ *Tamales de Elote*

These delicious tamales must be made when corn is in
season, but as they freeze like a dream, they can
be used all year.

3 ½ cups Quaker Masa
 Harina
2 cups warm water
¾ cup lard
2 tsp. salt
6 large ears fresh corn

1 ½ cups finely diced Jack
 cheese
1 4-oz. can peeled green
 chiles
Salt and pepper

*Prepare Masa Harina as for Turkey Tamales. Husk corn,
taking care not to split husks; discard silk and clip off
thick curved part at bottom of husks. Score each row of corn
kernels with a sharp knife, then scrape off corn with the
back of the knife. Mix with cheese. Rinse chiles, discarding
seeds, and chop. Combine with corn, and add salt and pepper
to taste. Spread prepared masa on the inside of 2 corn husks
which have been placed together, but in opposite directions
(point of one husk at top, the other at bottom). The masa
should cover the lower-middle section of the husks. Put
a spoonful of the corn-cheese mixture on the masa, fold sides
over to cover it, then carefully fold the filled section up
over the rest of the husk. This makes them open-ended, which
is typical of this type of tamale. Arrange in a steamer with
the fold at the bottom so the filling won't fall out. Cover
and steam 50 minutes. These make a wonderful vegetable to
serve with charcoal-broiled meat.*

BREADS, COOKIES, CAKES

FLOUR TORTILLAS
⇛ *Tortillas de Harina*

Tortillas made from masa are used in many of the
Mexican recipes I give in this book, but I see
no reason to give a recipe for home-made ones here, as
tortillas are obtainable almost everywhere in our
country, either fresh or canned. Less popular,
but delicious, are the flour tortillas which are easily
made. They are much better when made fresh
but may be reheated.

4 cups flour	1 to 1¼ cups lukewarm
2 tsp. salt	water
6 tbs. shortening	

*Sift flour and salt, work in the shortening, and stir in a
cup of water; then form a ball. If necessary you may use
more water until the bowl is clear of all dough. Knead
dough on lightly floured board and make into balls the size
of an egg. Let these stand about 15 minutes; then roll out
until they are the size of a salad plate. Bake on hot,
ungreased griddle or skillet for 2 minutes on one side, turn,
and cook about 1 minute on other side.*

⇛ Favorites in the north of Mexico, these tortillas
sometimes assume king-size proportions. We once
encountered service-plate-sized ones, and enjoyed every
inch.

97

ANISE ROLLS
 ⁊❧ *Molletes*

"El que hambre tiene en pan piensa."
"He who is hungry thinks of bread."

1 cup milk	*1 egg*
2 tsp. ground anise seed	*1 cake moist compressed*
2 tbs. lard or other	*yeast, softened in 2 tbs.*
shortening	*warm water*
⅓ cup sugar	*4¼ cups sifted flour*
1½ tsp. salt	

Scald the milk with the anise seed, then add shortening, sugar, and salt, and cool to lukewarm. Beat the egg slightly, and add with the yeast cake, which has been moistened in 2 tablespoons of warm water. Blend in the flour, mix well, cover, and allow to stand in a warm place until double in bulk—about an hour. Shape the dough into balls about the size of a golf ball, place 2 inches apart on a greased cookie sheet, and again allow to double in size. Brush lightly with melted shortening and bake at 400° for about 15 minutes, or until brown. This should yield about 2 dozen medium-sized rolls.

 ⁊❧ After tasting these feathery light sweet rolls, we organized the "Society for More Frequent Use of Anise Seed in American Cookery." Anise lends a subtle charm with its faint licorice flavor.

BUÑUELOS

Buñuelos are deep-fat-fried batter, usually sprinkled with cinnamon and sugar or with thin honey, but they may also be served plain. A favorite Mexican way of serving them is to break them into a large soup bowl and cover with a thin syrup of brown sugar flavored with stick cinnamon. Another type of

98

buñuelos, popular in Mexico, are made like rosettes in special iron molds which come apart to form different sizes and shapes.

4 cups sifted flour	1 tsp. salt
1 tbs. sugar (omit if these are to be used as bread)	2 eggs
	½ cup milk
1 tsp. baking powder	¼ cup melted butter

Sift together the flour, sugar, baking powder, and salt, then add the eggs, beaten with the milk, and the melted butter. Mix into a soft dough, turn out on a floured board, and knead until smooth. Divide the dough into walnut-sized pieces and rub each with a little shortening to prevent their sticking together. Cover with a cloth and let stand 20 minutes; then make each ball into a very thin, flat pancake, using a rolling pin if you are American, tortilla technique if Mexican. Let these stand a few minutes before frying in deep hot fat until puffed and brown.

ટ⁓ Elena laughingly says that in some parts of Mexico the women pat the buñuelos extra thin on their thighs. She doesn't recommend the practice. In Spanish a buñuelo can mean a failure—a flop, like a pancake, its culinary meaning. We feel certain you won't have a buñuelo with these buñuelos.

BUÑUELOS WITH MUSCATEL WINE

"Las penas con pan son menos."
"You worry less if you eat more."

These buñuelos are sweet and definitely a dessert bread.

2 cups sifted flour	2 tbs. shortening
2 tsp. sugar	2 egg yolks, beaten
1 tsp. salt	3 tbs. Muscatel wine

Mix together the flour, sugar, and salt; then stir in the shortening, beaten egg yolks, and wine. (Any dessert wine is fine.) Form all into a soft dough, and roll out on a floured board until very thin. Cut into strips (or diamonds, or whatever shape you wish) and fry in deep fat until golden. Drain on paper, and while still warm dust with powdered sugar or roll in a mixture of ½ cup sugar and 1 teaspoon of cinnamon. This makes about three dozen.

&⤳ As a prologue for this recipe, the above proverb seems to suit perfectly when translated literally: "Pains with bread are felt less." Certainly you will feel nothing but pleasure with *this* bread. We think you would like to try a wine-flavored syrup with these buñuelos.

FRIED BREAD PUFFS
&⤳ *Sopaipillas*

Famous in New Mexico, sopaipillas are often called buñuelos there, and, like buñuelos, can be served plain with soups or entrées, or as a sweet when sprinkled with sugar and cinnamon or honey. When fried they will look like little pillows. Good with guacamole for soups or salads.

2 cups sifted flour	2 tbs. lard or shortening
2 tsp. baking powder	½ cup water
1 tsp. salt	

Sift together the flour, baking powder, and salt, and work in the lard or other shortening, and the water. Proceed as in the buñuelo recipe, but roll the dough on a floured board and cut in squares, triangles, or diamonds. Deep-fry at 400°, at first pushing the fritters under the fat two or three times to assure even puffing. Cook on both sides until nicely browned and prettily puffed. This recipe makes about 20 sopaipillas.

&⤳ Puffed up with rightful pride, these deep-fried fritters serve as hot bread when butter is their mate, as dessert when doused with syrup. Wonderful to serve with any meal, sopaipillas offer an occasional change from tortillas, if you are having an all-Mexican food party.

BUTTER BALLS

"Bien cocina la moza, pero mejor la bolsa."
"The maid cooks well, but the pocketbook cooks better."

1 cup butter	*3 cups flour*
½ cup sugar	*1 tsp. baking powder*
2 egg yolks	*Extra butter*
1 tsp. vanilla	

CUSTARD FILLING

1 cup cream (or half and half)	*2 tbs. flour*
	2 tbs. sugar
2 egg yolks	*½ tsp. almond extract*
	Almonds or candied cherries

Cream butter and sugar together, add unbeaten egg yolks and vanilla; then the flour sifted with the baking powder. Mix all together, using the hands, until a smooth dough is formed. Chill thoroughly. Roll the dough into 18 little round balls, pressing the tops with the thumb to make a cavity in each. Place on a baking sheet, about 2 inches apart, and chill again. Meanwhile scald the cream, mix the egg yolks with flour, sugar, and flavoring, add to the hot cream, and cook slowly, stirring constantly, until thick and smooth (about 5 minutes). Cool custard, put a piece of butter the size of a pea in each cavity of the chilled pastry balls, fill with custard, and bake in a 350° oven about 15 or 20 minutes. These should be filled the same day they are baked.

&ᴥ Just pop one of these lucious little confections into your mouth, and blissfully close your eyes to cares and calories. Tomorrow is soon enough to diet. Better postpone it yet another day, and use those leftover egg whites for Elena's equally delicious little fruit pastries or her heavenly meringues.

LITTLE HONEYS

࿔ Ojaldrados

Take my advice and don't try these on your busiest
day, as their base is puff paste, which takes time.
I shan't take space to give you my puff pastry recipe,
as good ones are to be found in any cook book.

1 standard recipe for puff
pastry, using 2 cups flour
and 1⅓ cups butter

½ cup honey
1 tbs. powdered cinnamon

*Make a recipe for puff pastry. After the fourth and last
chilling, roll the dough into an oblong about 10 by 15
inches. Cut this into six 5-inch squares, fold the two
edges over to meet and slightly overlap in the center,
moistening edge with a little water to seal. Bake at 425° for
20 to 25 minutes, or until light brown. Cover each square
with honey which has been warmed and mixed
with the cinnamon.*

࿔ These rich little pastries are indeed
appropriately named, and delightful to serve at teatime,
or with a dish of simply prepared fruit for dessert.
They are well worth a bit of your time, but when
Elena, who has no fear of work, warns you of the labor
involved for puff pastry, 'tis best to take heed.

FRUIT PASTRIES

࿔ Pastelillos de Frutas

You must begin with puff pastry for these too, as for
the ojaldrados above, so allow yourself plenty of time.

1 standard recipe for puff
pastry
2 egg whites
Pinch of salt
½ cup of powdered sugar

½ cup chopped walnuts
½ cup seeded, chopped
raisins
½ cup moist cocoanut

*Beat the egg whites with salt until a soft peak is reached.
Gradually add powdered sugar and beat until stiff. Fold
in the walnuts, seeded raisins, and cocoanut. After the final
chilling of your puff paste, cut it into 24 squares, put a
large spoonful of the fruit mixture on each, and bake
at 300° for 20 minutes, or until a lovely brown.*

ह‍ঙ If you are scared off by puff pastry (it's really
fun!) we can't believe this recipe won't work out
beautifully with a rich plain pastry.

LITTLE NUT COOKIES

ह‍ঙ *Bizcochitos con Nueces*

Keep these easily made little cakes around for
unexpected guests. There is no house big enough for
two families, but there is always room for hospitality.

3 cups sifted flour	*½ cup milk*
⅓ cup sugar	*¼ cup melted butter*
1 tbs. baking powder	*Unbeaten egg white*
½ tsp. salt	*¼ cup sugar*
1 large egg, beaten	*½ cup finely chopped nuts*

*Sift together the flour, sugar, baking powder, and salt.
Make a hole in the middle of this mixture and add
the beaten egg, milk, and melted butter. Mix well and roll
out on a floured board a rectangle about ⅜ inch thick.
Shape, and brush the top of the dough with unbeaten egg
white. Sprinkle with the sugar and nuts, pressing
the nuts into the dough with a spatula. Cut into strips
approximately 3 by 1 inches and bake on a greased cookie
sheet at 400° for about 20 minutes, or until lightly
browned. You will get about 18 cookies.*

ह‍ঙ Just *try* to keep these around! They are a
particularly delightful accompaniment to fruit. Stewed
quinces would be nice, or mangoes. Did you know
that these fruits are now available in cans at most
fancy grocery stores? Very good, too.

LITTLE TEA WREATHS
&ev *Rosquitas para Te*

Wonderful to have around for the holidays, these little cookies can be attractively decorated. The green of chopped pistachio nuts makes them look like their name.

¼ cup sugar	2 cups sifted flour
½ cup butter	2 tsp. baking powder
1 tsp. grated orange rind	1 egg white
3 egg yolks	

Cream sugar and butter with orange rind, then add the unbeaten egg yolks. Sift the flour with the baking powder into the creamed mixture and stir to form a somewhat stiff dough. Turn out on a lightly floured board, roll ½ inch thick and cut with a doughnut cutter. Place the cookies on a baking sheet, brush with the unbeaten egg white, and bake at 375° until lightly browned (about 20 minutes). This amount makes about eight large cookies.

&ev Guests will find these dainties irresistible—as pretty to look at as they are delicious to taste. A good excuse to shine up the tea service.

DRUNKEN CUPCAKES
&ev *Bizcochos Borrachos*

CUPCAKES

1 whole egg	½ cup sugar
4 eggs, separated	¾ cup sifted flour
½ tsp. salt	Jam or preserves

SAUCE

½ cup water	⅓ cup brandy
½ cup sugar	

Beat the whole egg, the egg yolks, and the salt together
well, gradually adding the sugar. Fold in the flour and then
the stiffly beaten egg whites. Fill ungreased cupcake
pans about two-thirds full of batter and bake in preheated
350° oven for about 25 minutes. Turn the pans upside
down to cool. Remove from pans, place on serving dish, dot
each cake with a spoonful of jam. Boil water and sugar
together for 5 minutes, add brandy, and spoon this sauce
over each cake. These should stand about ½ hour
before serving. The recipe makes about a dozen and a half,
if they are small.

ह✍ "Para todo mal, mezcal, para todo bien, también."
"Brandy for sickness, brandy for health, also."

If you like babas au rhum you will really go for these!

SESAME SEED CAKE

CAKE

1½ cups sifted flour   ½ cup milk
2 tsp. baking powder   1 egg
¼ tsp. salt   3 tbs. melted butter
½ cup sugar

TOPPING

½ cup sifted flour   Pinch of salt
½ cup brown sugar   2 tbs. melted butter
½ tsp. cinnamon   2 tbs. sesame seed

Sift together the flour, baking powder, salt, and sugar.
Add the milk, egg, and butter, and stir until blended. Pour
batter into a well-greased 9-inch baking pan, cover with
topping made by blending all ingredients except the sesame
seed, which is sprinkled over the topping. Bake in a 350°
oven for 30 minutes. This makes eight servings.

ह✍ Here is our idea of a perfect coffee cake for a
glamorous Sunday morning breakfast. Easter morning,
perhaps, or should we wait that long?

TURNOVERS WITH SWEET FILLING
&~ *Empanadas de Dulce*

There is practically no limit to the fillings for empanadas. As popular in South and Central America as they are in Mexico, they may be served as an appetizer, an entrée, or as a dessert. They may be baked or fried, served hot or cold. I list them under appetizers, with unsweetened filling, as well as here.

Mix and roll a rich pie crust dough, using ⅔ cup of shortening to 2 cups of flour, and adding 2 tablespoons of sugar for these sweet-filled empanadas. If you wish to fry rather than bake them, be sure to cut your shortening to ½ cup. Cut the rolled pastry into about 3- or 4-inch rounds, place a spoonful of your preferred filling on each, wet the edges with water, and fold over, pressing the edges together. Bake in a 375° oven for 15 to 20 minutes, or deep-fat fry until golden. I like to roll them, while still hot, in sugar and cinnamon. This amount of pastry should make about a dozen empanadas. Here are suggested fillings:

I. Sweet potato and cocoanut: Make a syrup by boiling 1 cup of water with 2 cups of brown sugar. Pour over thin-sliced sweet potatoes (3 medium), sprinkle with ¾ can of shredded cocoanut and bake until liquid has been absorbed. Cool before filling empanadas. Drained, crushed pineapple and ground blanched almonds are excellent with sweet mashed potato, too.

II. Sweetened picadillo (p. 64) makes an empanada similar to a mincemeat tart.

III. Thick applesauce flavored with cinnamon.

IV. Simply your pet preserves or jam.

&~ As a dessert for a large party, these empanadas can't be beat, as they freeze beautifully, either before or after baking, and your guests may enjoy a variety of fillings. Make up more of your own. We discovered Jack cheese with quince or guava paste.

ST. HONORÉ CAKE

Do this on your day off, as it will take a little time, but you'll find it's more fun than buying a new hat. It is customary in France to serve this gorgeous cake with Champagne at christenings.

PASTRY

¼ lb. butter   1 cup flour
1 package cream cheese

FILLING

10 tbs. cornstarch   2 eggs
1 qt. milk   ¼ to ½ cup rum
1 cup sugar

CREAM PUFFS

4 tbs. butter   ½ cup flour
½ cup water   2 eggs

FOR ASSEMBLING AND GARNISH

1 cup whipped cream,   ½ cup caramelized sugar
   flavored with 2 tbs. sugar
   and 1 tbs. vanilla, Maraschino
   cherries or strawberries

The pastry is made by creaming together the butter and cheese, adding the flour, and shaping into a ball. Roll this out to ¼-inch thickness. (I pat it out with my hands.) Cut into a 12-inch circle (a pastry wheel is good for this), chill for 2 or 3 hours; then bake at 400° from 12 to 15 minutes.

For the cream puffs, put the butter and water in a saucepan and bring to a boil; then add the flour all at once. Stir until the dough is smooth and does not cling to the pan. Remove from fire, and add the unbeaten eggs, one at a time, stirring well after each. Make little puffs (about 22) on a baking sheet, and bake at 425° until puffed; then reduce heat to 350° and finish baking until the puffs are dry enough to hold their shape. (If in doubt, take out one

and test it.) Total baking time should be 25 to 30 minutes.
When cold make a tiny slit on one side near the base
and fill with the rum filling, which is made like this:
Dissolve the cornstarch in a small amount of the milk. Heat
the remaining milk with sugar; then thicken with
cornstarch mixture. Beat the eggs and add some of the milk
mixture to the eggs, stirring well. Then add the eggs to
the remaining milk mixture. Cook, stirring, for 2 or 3
minutes. Remove from fire and add rum.

Now for assembling the cake: Place the baked pastry on
plate on which it is to be served. Put 18 of the filled cream
puffs around the edge of the pastry, and 4 in the center.
Dip the base of each puff in caramelized sugar before you
place it on the pastry. This will hold the puffs in place.
Sugar is caramelized by melting it slowly in a heavy pan
until it liquefies. Keep it in a pan of boiling water to keep
from hardening as you work. Put the remainder of the
filling on the pastry, and cover in patterned swirls with
whipped cream in a pastry tube. Decorate each puff with a
cherry or a strawberry, first dipped in the caramelized
sugar so it will stick to the puff.

३❧ Elena's inclusion of this very French and very
famous pastry is yet another tribute to her talents as a
cook and her dauntlessness as a person. This tricky
business may faze some of you sighted cooks, but
leaves Elena unflurried.

Desserts

FRITTERS IN SYRUP
ᘒ *Torrejas*

Spain is the origin of this recipe, where, in certain parts, it is customary to serve this on the day a new baby is born into the household.

6 eggs, separated
1 cup fine cake crumbs, any
stale cake, preferably
pound
½ cup butter

1 cup sugar
2 cups water
1 medium stick cinnamon
Raisins and almonds

Beat the whites of eggs until stiff, adding the yolks one by one and beating after each addition. Add the cake crumbs and mix thoroughly. Heat the butter, drop the batter in by spoonfuls, and fry until the fritters are golden brown on both sides. Drain on absorbent paper, while making a light syrup by boiling together the water and sugar with the cinnamon stick. Boil the fritters in the syrup for 5 minutes and allow to cool in it. When cold, garnish the serving platter with almonds and raisins. Makes about a dozen.

ᘒ What a pity the guest of honor is too young to enjoy this wondrous treat!

ALMOND DESSERT

 ৯ *Almendrado*

Very "fiesta" indeed is this pretty tricolored dessert.
The recipe given here will serve eight persons with a
party menu, but fewer if your food is less elaborate.

DESSERT

1 envelope unflavored gelatin	¾ cup sugar
¼ cup cold water	1 tsp. almond extract
¾ cup boiling water	Green and red food coloring
5 egg whites	½ cup blanched almonds,
¼ tsp. salt	chopped coarsely

CUSTARD

1½ cups milk, scalded	1 tsp. vanilla
5 egg yolks	Dash of salt
½ cup cold milk	

*Soften gelatin in cold water for 5 minutes, then dissolve
in boiling water, and chill until mixture begins to thicken.
Beat the egg whites with salt until stiff. Add sugar
gradually, beating until mixture stands up in nice peaks.
Beat in the chilled gelatin, almond extract, and one half of
the almonds. Divide this mixture into three equal parts,
leaving one white, tinting one green, the other pink.
Sprinkle the remaining almonds over the bottom of a wet
mold or loaf pan (about 2-quart capacity). Spread first the
green layer, then the white layer, and last, the pink layer
in the mold. Chill until firm, unmold, and serve with
custard sauce made as follows: Beat the egg yolks with ½
cup of cold milk, sugar, vanilla, and salt. Gradually stir
into the scalded milk, and cook over hot water until the
mixture coats a metal spoon. Pour at once into a cold
bowl and chill before serving. Serves six.*

 ৯ A little stretch of the imagination on that pink
coloring (or a little intensification of same) would
make the Mexican flag colors. What a flattering and

memorable dessert to serve at a party for an arriving dignitary *from* Mexico, or a departing dignitary *to* Mexico!

ALMOND TORTE
ใ๛ *Torta de Almendra*

Originally Spanish, this dessert has become very familiar to Mexicans. This keeps fresh for quite a while, if you can keep it from the family.

9 eggs, separated	¾ lb. ground almonds
1½ cups sugar	(unblanched!)
Peel of a large lemon, grated	Pinch of salt

Beat the egg yolks well with the sugar. Add ground almonds and mix thoroughly; then the grated lemon peel. Lastly fold in the egg whites, whipped stiff but not dry with salt. Bake in a well-buttered pan in 400° oven for 30 to 45 minutes. A spring mold is ideal for this. Serves eight to ten persons. This dessert looks pretty when garnished with blanched almonds to form daisy petals, with raisins for centers.

ใ๛ Moist, rich, delectable, and nice to make when eggs are cheap.

POUND CAKE AND CHEESE DESSERT
ใ๛ *Postre de Mamón*

This dessert is famous in Mexico, and is served in one or another of its variations in practically every household during the Lenten season.

1½ cups water	3 oz. brandy
1¾ cups sugar	8 slices of pound cake
2 tbs. butter	½ lb. Monterey Jack cheese
4 eggs, separated	Cinnamon to taste

111

Make a syrup by boiling sugar and water together for about 3 minutes. Melt the butter in the syrup and add the beaten yolks of eggs, then the brandy, and last, the stiffly beaten whites. Butter a fairly shallow ovenproof dish, and cover the bottom with sliced pound cake covered with slices of the cheese. Bathe with the syrup mixture, and repeat in layers until all cake and cheese have been used. Have the syrup and egg mixture covering the top of the dish. Bake in a 325° oven until set. Sprinkle generously with cinnamon, and serve either warm or cold, but warm is far preferable, as the cheese should be soft. This amount should serve six, but it seldom does!

܅ This daring but happy combination of cheese and syrup will surprise and delight you. It is Elena's inspired version of the well-known capirotada, or Mexican bread pudding, which also features cheese, and sometimes even tomatoes and onions in the syrup! True to form, Elena has adapted this divinely to the American palate. Mexicans love very sweet desserts and so does Elena, but should you wish, home-made bread (or a reasonable facsimile) tastes just as good as the cake. Who minds Lent?

COCOANUT TRIFLE
"Bien me sabe."
"It tastes good to me."

1 ¾ cups milk	*¼ cup sifted flour*
¾ cup moist shredded	*2 egg whites*
cocoanut (fresh or canned)	*¼ cup sugar*
2 egg yolks	*½ tsp. vanilla extract*
¼ cup milk	*6 slices of sponge cake*
⅓ cup sugar	*¼ cup shredded cocoanut*

Heat milk with ¾ cup of cocoanut in the top of a double boiler over hot water until the milk is scalded. Beat the egg yolks slightly, and mix until smooth with ¼ cup of

112

milk, ⅓ cup of sugar, and the sifted flour. Pour this
mixture gradually into the hot milk, and cook over hot
water, stirring constantly until smooth and just thickened
(about 10 minutes). Be sure the water in the bottom of the
double boiler is kept boiling. Place the slices of sponge
cake in the bottom of a serving dish, and pour the
hot custard over them. Make a meringue by beating the egg
whites to a soft peak, adding the sugar and flavoring,
and continue beating until stiff. Cover the dish with
meringue; sprinkle with the ¼ cup of cocoanut and place
in a moderate oven until slightly browned on top.
Serve this cold to six.

ঽ৵ Our old friend—all done up with cocoanut.

CARAMEL-COATED CUSTARD
ঽ৵ *Flan*

Flan is the most typical of the Spanish desserts
extended to the Americas, and perhaps the most
popular. For this reason I repeat the recipe for the
vanilla-flavored flan which appeared in my other book
also, but in addition give here some of the many
delicious variations.

1 ¾ cups sugar	2 tall cans evaporated milk
3 egg whites	2 tsp. vanilla extract
8 egg yolks	6 tbs. brandy or rum

*Put 1 cup of sugar into a deep pan in which the custard
is to be baked, and place it over the fire, stirring constantly
until the sugar melts and turns golden. Tip the pan
around until it is entirely coated with the caramel, then
cool while making the custard. Beat the whites and
egg yolks together, add milk, remaining sugar, and vanilla,
mixing well. Strain into the coated pan, cover, and place
pan in a larger pan containing hot water. (In Spanish this
is called a "baño de María" or "Mary's bath.") Bake in
a 350° oven for about 1 hour, or until a knife inserted in*

the center comes out clean. *Allow to cool somewhat,
but turn out on a platter while still warm, or the caramel
will not come loose from the pan. When ready to serve,
pour brandy or rum over the flan and send to the
table burning. Serves eight to ten. Flans are at their best
when made hours before serving and thoroughly chilled.*

Variations:

ORANGE FLAN: *Make as above, substituting orange juice
for the milk, 1 tsp. grated orange rind for the vanilla,
and adding 2 egg yolks more. This will probably take a
longer cooking time, as will the pineapple flan.*

COCOANUT FLAN: *To basic recipe add ½ cup of grated
cocoanut cooked in ½ cup of water until transparent.*

ALMOND FLAN: *Add ¼ pound of blanched, ground
almonds to basic recipe.*

PINEAPPLE FLAN: *Use basic recipe, substituting pineapple
juice for the milk, and adding 2 egg yolks.*

Ⳕ Glamour girl of desserts, Elena's flan has become
almost as famous as Elena herself to the many who
have dined at her bountiful table. Ethereal food, simple
to make, gorgeous to behold! Pick your flavor, they
are all divine.

OLD-FASHIONED MEXICAN DESSERT
Ⳕ *Postre Antiguo*

Many of the old Mexican recipes for desserts were
made centuries ago by nuns in convents and have been
passed on down the years with little or no changes
from the originals. They were called "platters," and are
still served that way.

¾ cup sugar	5 egg yolks
4 whole cloves	½ lb. of pound cake
1 cup water	Maraschino cherries and
½ cup Sherry wine	canned figs for garnish

*Boil the sugar and cloves in water for 5 minutes. Remove
from fire and add Sherry. Moisten the sliced pound cake
with this syrup and place the slices on a platter. Add the
slightly beaten egg yolks to the remaining syrup, and
return to the fire, stirring the mixture constantly until it
coats the spoon. Pour over the sliced cake and garnish
with cherries and figs or any chosen fruit. Berries are
nice, too. Serve warm or cold to six.*

&⤳ Paradoxically, these popular Mexican desserts,
made from pouring syrup over a sponge- or pound-
cake base, are still known by the name "ante," although
they certainly are not served *before* the meal.

PINEAPPLE MILK DESSERT
&⤳ *Arequipa de Piña*

In Mexico thick, sweet desserts are served in very small
portions to finish off the meal with a sweet taste.
This rich dessert is thick—almost like the famous
cajeta, which is thick enough to be packed in a little
wooden box, whence it gets its name. I find this
Arequipa is best when kept for 5 or 6 days and then
served at room temperature.

1 qt. milk
1½ cups sugar
*¼ cup ground, blanched
  almonds*

1 tsp. cornstarch
*1 cup crushed, drained
  pineapple*

*Add 1 cup of sugar to the milk, almonds, and cornstarch,
and cook slowly until it starts to thicken. Put in the
remainder of the sugar and the pineapple, and continue
cooking until the bottom of the pan can be seen when
stirring. Remember, it should be thick, and it requires long
cooking. Pour it onto a platter to cool.*

115

ह‍ Arequipa, province and city in Peru founded in 1540 by Pizarro, produced the original formula which has served as a model all these years for the many variations of this sweet. Forgive the historical digression but we find it fascinating that this dessert has preserved its original identity after so many years of Mexican adaptation. After eating this, you will agree with us that a sweet tooth is standard equipment for a Mexican.

MERINGUES WITH SOUR CREAM AND BROWN SUGAR

This is nothing more than simple meringues with a little different topping, which my guests find delightful. If you have a favorite meringue recipe, by all means use it. I include one here which is enough to make a dozen large meringues.

3 egg whites	*1 cup sugar*
Pinch of cream of tartar	*1 tsp. vanilla or lemon extract*
Pinch of salt	

Beat the egg whites very stiff with the cream of tartar and salt, then beat in the sugar gradually, until the mixture stands up in peaks. Add flavoring and drop by tablespoons onto a well-buttered baking sheet. Wet the spoon and make a nest in the top of each meringue, then bake in a very slow oven (250°) for 30 minutes. After they are baked and cooled, put on a nice gob of sour cream, sweetened with brown sugar, and dash with grated nutmeg or cinnamon.

ह‍ Who was it said, "The best things in life are the simple things?" This time we agree. For heavenly eating, try these with poached fruit on the side. Maybe quinces?

116

PANCAKES WITH COTTAGE CHEESE

These are a real treat, and nice to serve alone
or with fruit.

7 eggs, separated   *1 lb. cottage cheese*
7 tbs. flour (level)   *Salt to taste*

 Beat the egg yolks, add the flour, cottage cheese, and salt,
then fold in the stiffly beaten whites of eggs. Fry as you
would pancakes and serve hot with powdered sugar and
cinnamon, or better, with warmed honey and
cinnamon. Serves four.

 &this; Chafing dish owners should have fun
experimenting with this easier variation of a crepe. Try
rolling half a banana in each pancake and setting
all ablaze with brandy.

PEARS AND QUINCE IN CLARET SAUCE

It's too bad that quinces are not used more often—they
cook up so beautifully. (Try adding them to an apple
pie sometime.) However, if quinces are unavailable,
use green apples with pears, or peaches which are not
quite ripe; or peaches with apples. They are all good.

1 large quince   *1 cup claret*
4 pears (not fully ripened) *4 tbs. lemon juice*
2 tbs. butter   *6 strips lemon peel*
1½ cups sugar

 Parboil the quince for 10 minutes, then cool, peel, and
cut into 6 sections. Peel and core the pears and cut
into quarters. Sauté the fruit in the hot butter very gently
until light brown. Heat the sugar with the claret and
lemon peel, and simmer the fruit in this syrup until just
soft, but not mushy, from 15 to 25 minutes, depending on
the firmness of the pears. Add the lemon juice and
serve the fruit either hot or cold with the claret sauce in
which it was simmered. Enough for six.

117

ც A triumphant finale to a hearty meal! Serve these ambrosial fruits pridefully—a dish to please the most fastidious diner.

PRESSED QUINCE PASTE
ც *Cajeta de Membrillo*

Typically Mexican, this takes time to prepare, but will keep indefinitely. Once done, you have in reserve an emergency dessert, perfect with cheese, to finish a meal. Guava and mango pastes are made in the same manner.

Wash the quinces and steam until tender—about 20 minutes. Cut in quarters, removing core and seeds. (I have learned it's much easier to core and seed after steaming.) Grind through the finest blade of your food chopper, skin and all. Measure out your quince pulp and add an equal amount of sugar. Mix well and place in a pot that is easy to hold on to, as you are going to do a lot of stirring. Use a wooden spoon and stir constantly, as the mixture cooks, or it will burn. When the mixture is quite thick, and you can see the bottom of the pan clearly, empty it into a square or oblong pan and cool. When cold the cooked quince is turned out on a wax paper covered board, covered with cheesecloth, and placed in the sun for 2 days. Turn the board around occasionally to expose all surfaces to the sun, as this treatment prevents molding. Store the pressed quince covered, in a cool, dry place.

ც A gourmet's delight, and the perfect accompaniment to most any after-dinner cheese. We drool to think of this sweet with our great pet of cheeses, Teleme. Take note of that sun treatment, and scan the weather predictions before embarking on this project.

118

FIESTA FRUIT PLATTER

This platter lends itself to practically any variation of fruits: fresh or canned pineapple, bananas, and other kinds of melons are equally delicious. Select according to your taste and what is in season, but beg or borrow a glass pitcher for that beautifully colored raspberry juice.

3 cups raspberries (frozen
    or fresh)
1 cup sugar (unless
    sweetened, frozen berries
    are used)
2 (3-oz.) packages of
    cream cheese
¼ cup cream

3 peaches, peeled and sliced
9 to 12 apricots, peeled
    and halved
9 to 12 figs, peeled and
    halved
2 to 3 cups melon balls (I use
    cantaloupe or Persian)

Combine the raspberries and sugar, let stand an hour or so, then mash and force through a sieve. Pour this sauce into your glass pitcher. Mash the cream cheese and beat with the cream until smooth and fluffy. Put this mixture in a small serving bowl. Arrange the fruits on a large platter, and serve accompanied by the raspberry sauce and the cream cheese topping. For six or eight.

ॐ You are the artist here, so let your imagination and your talents run rampant with Nature's beautiful fruits.

"Ayúdate y Dios te ayudará."
"God helps those who help themselves."

PEACHES SUPREME

When in season, fresh, peeled peach halves are delightful in place of the canned. This recipe is right for 4 to 5 whole peaches. One half peach is usually enough to serve each guest. Pineapple juice, or any fruit juice, may be used to pour over the fresh peaches before baking.

6 or 8 canned peach halves, drained
½ lb. macaroons (usually a dozen)

3 eggs, separated
3 tbs. powdered sugar
Juice from peaches, or other fruit juice

Beat the egg yolks with powdered sugar until creamy, fold in the crumbled macaroons, and then the stiffly beaten egg whites. Fill the peach halves with this mixture, and place in a pan, pour in some of the peach juice, and bake until lightly browned (15 to 20 minutes) in a 350° oven. Serve with whipped cream to six.

ફ≈ Of course we all know that lemon juice sprinkled over peeled fresh peaches helps retain their color, plus adding to their flavor. We have found that the mashed kernel of a fresh peach adds something here too. Just a suggestion.

BRANDIED STRAWBERRY SPONGE

1 sponge cake (not over 1½ in. thick)
4 baskets of strawberries
½ cup brandy

Sugar
Whipped cream sweetened with powdered sugar

Wash and hull berries. Slice half the amount of strawberries. Add sugar to taste and the brandy. Let stand in refrigerator about 1 hour. Add sugar to remaining whole berries and chill. Slit the cake lengthwise. Cover lower half with strawberries. Place top slice over this. Add remaining brandied strawberries, if any, and whole strawberries. Decorate with whipped cream sweetened with powdered sugar. The number served will depend on the size of the sponge cake used.

index

121

123

126

Other Ward Ritchie Press
COOKBOOKS

THE ART OF ORIENTAL COOKING: JAPANESE-CHINESE-KOREAN. By Mrs. Jung Suck Choy. $4.95

A BOOK OF APPETIZERS. By Helen Evans Brown, with a number of drinks by Philip S. Brown. $3.50

THE BOOK OF CURRIES AND CHUTNEYS. By William B. Templeton Veach, with Helen Evans Brown. $4.50

CHAFING DISH BOOK. By Helen Evans Brown. $3.50

THE COOKOUT BOOK, with an Introduction to Barbecue Cooking and Entertaining by Helen Evans Brown and Philip S. Brown. $5.95
16 full-page color photographs; 55 other illus.

CONSTANTINE COOKS THE GREEK WAY. [By Constantine Hassalevris]. $3.95

THE FOOD AND DRINK OF MEXICO. By George C. Booth. Illus. $5.95

FOOD FOR THE EMPEROR. Recipes of Imperial China, with a Dictionary of Chinese Cuisine, by John D. Keys. $4.95

THE HIGHLANDER'S COOKBOOK. Recipes from Scotland, by Sheila MacNiven Cameron. Illustrations by Mario Casetta. $5.95

[*continued on next page*]

I LOVE TO COOK BOOK. By Ruth Bateman. $5.00

ITALY ON A PLATTER. Recipes for Gourmets. By Osborne
   Putnam Stearns. Illus. $5.95

PATIO COOK BOOK. By Helen Evans Brown. $3.50

PHEASANTS FOR PEASANTS. By Selena Royle and George
   Renavent.   Paper $1.95

RECIPES FROM THE MELTING POT. International Cuisine.
   By Pam and Charles Nicolai. Illus. $4.95

SOMETHING SPECIAL COOK BOOK. By Ruth Mellinkoff,
   with illustrations by the author. $5.00

THE VIRGINIA CITY COOK BOOK. (Authentic Recipes of
   the Old West.) By Helen Evans Brown, Philip S. Brown,
   Katharine Best, and Katharine Hillyer. Illustrated by Harry
   O. Diamond, with a foreword by Lucius Beebe.
                        Gift edition $3.95 — Paper $1.95